Burn Your Ch

T0041014

Burn Your Chair

*Healing Chronic Pain
Through Active Rest*

Ari Heart

Toplight
Jefferson, North Carolina

All illustrations are by Kristen Jussila,
www.kristen-jussila.com.

LIBRARY OF CONGRESS CATALOGUING-IN-PUBLICATION DATA

Names: Heart, Ari, author.
Title: Burn your chair : healing chronic pain through active rest / Ari Heart.
Description: Jefferson, North Carolina : McFarland & Company, Inc.,
Publishers, 2022 | Includes bibliographical references and index.
Identifiers: LCCN 2021061108 | ISBN 9781476686165
(paperback : acid free paper) ∞
ISBN 9781476645674 (ebook)
Subjects: LCSH: Posture. | Chronic pain—Alternative treatment. |
Self-care, Health. | BISAC: SPORTS & RECREATION / Football
Classification: LCC RA781.5 .H43 2022 | DDC 613.7/8—dc23/eng/20211230
LC record available at https://lccn.loc.gov/2021061108

BRITISH LIBRARY CATALOGUING DATA ARE AVAILABLE

ISBN (print) 978–1-4766–8616–5
ISBN (ebook) 978–1-4766–4567–4

© 2022 Ari Heart. All rights reserved

*No part of this book may be reproduced or transmitted in any form
or by any means, electronic or mechanical, including photocopying
or recording, or by any information storage and retrieval system,
without permission in writing from the publisher.*

Front cover illustrations by Kristen Jussila

Printed in the United States of America

Toplight is an imprint of McFarland & Company, Inc., Publishers

*Box 611, Jefferson, North Carolina 28640
www.toplightbooks.com*

To Mel for inspiring this book and working
tirelessly to see it come to fruition.

To Mali for your unwavering support
and unconditional love.

To Joy for being the world's greatest yoga teacher.

Table of Contents

Table of Contents

Preface

"For all its material advantages, sedentary life has left us edgy and unfulfilled; even after 400 genera-tions in villages and cities, we haven't forgotten: the open road still softly calls like a nearly forgotten song of childhood."
—Carl Sagan

When we were kids, my sister and I spent hours playing outside. We'd climb the tree in our front yard, explore the old barn filled with amazing junk, chase our cats around the house, and play hide and seek in the attic. We knelt in the dirt in search of critters, squatted over streams looking for rocks to skip, and collapsed on the ground laughing when we were tired. I remember lying in my bed completely exhausted from the day's adventures, trying desperately to stay awake so that I could continue enjoying the bliss of relaxing after all that fun.

Then the screens came. It started with a seemingly harmless antenna TV that only picked up three stations, yet suddenly, our lives were forever changed. Instead of playing outside after school, we rushed home to our new electronic god and tuned into *Home Improvement*, a sitcom about a not-so-handy handyman. When the five o'clock news replaced the slapstick comedy with current events, we whined in defeat, unsure of what to do with ourselves until *Friends* came on at seven.

Soon a digitalized world overtook us. Classmates talked about *Hammertime* and NSYNC, and I thought they were going on about a new episode of *Home Improvement* I hadn't seen yet. We hounded our mom until she bought us cable TV so we too could study up on MTV. Next we begged for a Super Nintendo and *Super Mario World.*

Preface

When we outgrew the little Italian plumber and his dinosaur drama, we cried for a computer so we could learn about sex from the experts.

The screens became our babysitters. Pushing the power button on our devices as we burst through the door after school was a great relief, a ritual that released us from the torture of navigating our pubescent bodies. For our single mother it was a real money saver; no need for childcare or after-school programs. The cartoons and celebrities kept us well educated on what toys we needed to be cool and which foods would make us feel "*Grrreat!*"

But when Mom didn't have the money or see the benefit in supporting our childish cravings, she became the enemy. These were dark times in our single-parent home. If my sister and I weren't slumped on the couch in front of the TV or computer, we were standing in front of the refrigerator eating handfuls of shredded cheese and rolled-up lunch meat. We grew heavy, adding to the awkwardness of our rapidly changing bodies, and compounding the emotional pain and ridicule we traversed during our terrible teens.

In high school, we made a seamless transition from food and screens to drugs and alcohol. With our brains already conditioned to receive the instant gratification that sugar and flickering lights produce, substance abuse seemed like a second home. Addiction turned us from straight A students into sub-par slackers who would just barely squeak by our graduation requirements. Living like this left our bodies depressed and our minds dysfunctional and led to a cycle of chronic pain and disease we would struggle to break free from for the rest of our lives.

Shortly after I graduated high school, I awoke one morning to a disturbing sound: "*Fbbbt ... fbbbt ... fbbbt....*" It was as if someone were rhythmically blowing raspberries, but there was no laughter joining these typically playful sounds. "Please, someone help!" cried my mom's fiancé John from the next room. I peered across the hall to see my mother lying lifeless on the floor beside her bed, her lips sputtering each time John performed a CPR chest compression.

The death of my mother was the crux of my life and triggered my sister's life-altering schizophrenia. Healthy grieving practices were not a tradition in our family, so we turned to the only friends who had never let us down: food, drugs, and screens. Seeking asylum, my sister fled our family home to embark on a manic couch-surfing tour that would eventually leave her homeless. Falling into a downward spiral of self-abuse, I began bingeing on processed foods and all-night pill-fueled video game marathons.

I developed a crushing physical anxiety that I had no tools to cope with. Each time I thought about my late mother or my lost sister, my low back would lock up and burn with searing tension. I became serious and melancholy, a big change for the kid known for his Donald Duck and Mickey Mouse impressions. I buried thoughts of my family underneath habitually folded arms, furrowed brow, and hunched shoulders. Every day I pushed the image of my mother out of my mind so I wouldn't have to face my feelings. Soon I couldn't recall her face without a picture. I was the Eeyore of the group wherever I went. Tension from my anxiety attacks radiated into every muscle in my body, leading to chronic pain and eventually sciatica. I felt like a prisoner in my own body.

Finally, I met my breaking point. The signals my body was sending me were too loud to ignore. I realized that if I stayed inside on one more beautiful day hunched over a screen, I would only feel more decrepit and miserable than before. I knew it was time to make drastic changes if I hoped to escape the toxic cycle I had created. I flushed my drugs, sold my video games, and bought a gym membership.

Getting started was hard. I was never an athlete and had no idea what I was doing in the gym. The first few weeks were so uncomfortable that I wasn't sure I could continue. But the hole in my life created by ditching bad habits needed to be filled. After a few months of pushing myself to go to the gym every day, I began to feel a sense of normalcy that I hadn't felt since childhood. The endorphins from my workouts made me feel like a different person, lighter, less burdened. The natural antidepressants and painkillers of the exercise high replaced my drug habit without the nasty side effects.

Soon I started to see progress. My folded arms were a little bigger, new veins popped up, and I noticed myself standing a bit taller. When I would run into old friends from high school, they'd say, "Wow, I hardly recognize you!" Yet even though my muscles were growing, my heart remained the same size. I still wasn't happy. I couldn't fully pull myself out of the hole I had been hiding in. Toxic thought patterns always returned once the post-workout buzz wore off, and so too did the physical pain that accompanied them.

It seemed my uneducated style of exercising was great for building biceps, but it was also compounding the crippling tension growing in my body.

I started to feel bored with the gym. At the time, mixed martial arts was all the rage, and I had been watching the Ultimate Fighting Championship a lot. I was bullied and physically attacked for being overweight as a teenager, so the idea of learning to defend myself was intriguing. One day a friend at work invited me to come train at his brother's underground MMA club.

After one class, I was hooked. Through discipline I found the type of healthy consistency I needed all my life. I regained the body awareness I had lost when the screens became my friends. The repeated drills of fluid movements and focus on technique over brute force brought me a newfound sense of self-control. Every movement I made began to feel different. I noticed myself walking differently, bending over to pick things up differently, and even falling into bed differently. I felt instincts compelling me to bob, weave, and somersault through everyday life. The awkward, overweight teenager I still identified as swelled with pride, seeing all I was capable of. Exercise was freeing me from the traps I had laid for myself with an unhealthy lifestyle. I felt a sense of confidence and well-being that I hadn't experienced in years. And I was hungry for more. I wanted to keep getting better so that I could share the healing effects of movement with others. I decided to leave my cooking job and return to school to pursue a degree in exercise science with the intention of one day becoming a physical therapist.

Through martial arts I had learned a lot about moving my body, but I still didn't know much about self-care. Long periods of sitting at the computer to apply for college and financial aid and to study for the SAT inflamed my sciatica. Every time I would sit for an extended time, white-hot tingles shot down my left leg. My shoulders and neck felt rigid and immobile. I visited the massage therapist and chiropractor religiously seeking relief, but everything I tried felt like putting a Band-Aid on a broken arm. Unfortunately, modern martial arts systems replace the traditional focus on flexibility and mobility with more drilling of technique, so I had no idea what to do with my battered body outside of practice. The tension I was carrying combined with the rough-and-tumble nature of the martial arts

I practiced led to various injuries. I repeatedly tore the cartilage in my knees, tweaked my shoulders, and suffered from periodic lock-jaw and a deviated septum which inhibited my ability to breathe. To get me back to training, my doctors prescribed surgeries. Surgeries meant being reinjured in order to heal as well as more long periods of sitting while waiting for recovery, which started the cycle of pain all over again.

One day a training partner overheard me airing my frustrations with chronic pain and suggested I try stretching. When I first started, I couldn't touch my toes. Again, I had no idea what I was doing. It all felt so foreign, uncomfortable, and boring to my untrained mind. It was a no-brainer to combine my love of lazing around watching TV with my newfound curiosity of stretching. At the time, I was living with my father. His house had lots of open space and soft carpets. Every night when he flopped onto the couch to watch a movie, I'd sit on the floor and start stretching.

Soon I realized that I wasn't watching the TV anymore. It's hard to pay attention to anything else with your legs behind your head! I had unintentionally let go of my typical way of resting and began creating a more active form of recovery from the injuries and tension that compiled over the years. I felt more comfortable on the floor than on the plush sofas and rediscovered my youthful desire to explore physical sensations. For the first time in my life I dedicated myself to a daily practice of self-care. I noticed that relieving physical tension seemed to ameliorate my depression and anxiety. I was so elated the first time I touched my toes that I woke my father up in the middle of the night to tell him. Within a year, I was completely free of sciatica.

Shortly after I left for college my father killed himself. His suicide note revealed that he had been suffering from inexplicable body pain and tension. He felt powerless against my sister's disease, and it was weighing heavily on him. He had become addicted to painkillers and could no longer endure. It was a familiar story. Tension, addiction, and disconnection from my body were at least partially inherited traits. Like old friends vying for my attention, anxiety and toxic thoughts rushed back to attack me. "Maybe if I stayed, he'd still be alive," I thought. "If I had taken better care of my sister, he wouldn't have had to worry." My body and mind began to seize up again, and the urge to fall back on old habits was strong. The cycle was starting all over again.

Thankfully, my passion for fitness and the progress I had made in martial arts kept me moving forward. I became the instructor for the college's martial arts club and discovered a newfound passion for helping others overcome their pain and problems through movement, like I had. Teaching was the most rewarding thing I had ever done. I was sharing something that changed my life with people who were searching for the same. This made me question whether or not I really wanted to become a physical therapist. After spending a lot of time in hospitals rehabbing from surgeries, the idea of working in one the rest of my life was very unappealing. I wondered if there was another way I could combine my passions with my career. Since I loved teaching so much, a friend suggested I attend a yoga teacher training. I jumped at the chance. It seemed like the perfect complement to my new dream of opening a martial arts studio. "The *yin* to my *yang*," I thought. I had no experience with yoga, but I thought, "it's just stretching. I know how to stretch." The journey of transformation to follow was beyond anything I could have imagined.

Yoga saved my life. It taught me how to confront my pain, how to sit with it, how to accept it, and how to let it go. It offered me answers for both my physical and emotional pain. Through yoga I learned that my pain was much like the setting sun; the longer I stared at it, the more it would fade. Those uncomfortable sensations and emotions may return each day with a burning heat, but I always have the power to sit and watch the sun set again. When I started doing yoga, I would often break down crying after a practice. At first I didn't understand why I was crying, but I had an intuition that these were healing tears. During meditation I saw glimpses of my mother's face, I felt myself transported to the psyche ward to hug my sister, and I experienced every ounce of anguish that led my father to take his own life. I learned to allow myself the space to feel what I had been blocking out and to give myself the time I needed to let it go.

Soon I began to find new realms of possibility in my body. I could scratch that spot between my shoulder blades that I could never reach before. I could sit and stand for long periods of time without an aching back or tingling leg. I started experimenting with movement just for fun, just to explore. I felt such joy attempting headstands and handstands, experiencing the type of play I left behind long ago for reruns of *Home Improvement.*

As my college graduation approached and I started mechanically looking at schools of physical therapy, I knew I wasn't on the right path. The physical therapists who had helped me recover from my knee surgeries were very knowledgeable, but they spent most of their days locked away in hospital basements regurgitating the same exercise protocols over and over again. They had done nothing to provide me with tools that would help me finally break the cycle of pain in my life since the exercises only worked my quadriceps and left the rest of me unaddressed.

Considering the transformation I experienced, I wondered if yoga therapy was an established practice. A quick Google search led me to YouTube videos of yoga therapists working modern-day miracles. People were going to yoga therapists for everything from back pain to post-traumatic stress. Yoga therapists were able to offer their clients a more holistic healing plan, a plan that addressed the client's entire life rather than treating them like cars with faulty parts that needed mending. One video stopped me in my tracks. It followed an elderly man who was walking into a yoga therapist's office hunched over like Quasimodo. Before entering, he said, "I go in a question mark," while staring at the ground. When he came out he proclaimed, "and I leave an exclamation point!" He looked like a totally different person. He stood tall and smiled with his whole body, looking straight ahead instead of sadly looking down. Even his voice sounded different! I knew I had found my calling.

About This Book

The practices presented in this book came to me as I began my training to become a yoga therapist. The Phoenix Rising Yoga Therapy training center in Bristol, Vermont, was in the basement of an old apartment building. Unlike the basement of a hospital or another typical gym filled with equipment, it was just a big open space for movement finished with carpet that was soft and plush, much like my father's home where I first discovered self-care. It was more inviting than a typical classroom because instead of desks and chairs there were bolsters, blocks, and blankets for creating a new nest to work and rest from each day.

At first I found it a bit obtuse and uncomfortable to sit on the floor all day to complete my work, as I had spent my entire academic career sitting at a desk. I found it awkward trying to take notes or stay attentive sitting on the floor. Many of my peers opted to sit in the few metal folding chairs in the room that were there to help modify yoga postures for people who have trouble getting down to the floor. But I knew all too well the pain that awaited me in those chairs, so I refused to conform.

After a few days of experimenting with sitting on the floor, I discovered that if I were mindful of my comfort level and how it correlated with my posture, that I could shift my posture or the items supporting me to relieve any pain. I noticed that by utilizing the active rest postures I had learned from previous yoga training, I was able to remain more engaged in my studies while also addressing the tension in my body.

One of the first concepts we learned about in our training was *the edge*, the place in which we are uncomfortable but know intuitively that we stand to benefit from the discomfort in some way, like the discomfort you experience during a deep tissue massage. I was recovering from my third knee surgery at the time, so kneeling or sitting cross-legged felt incredibly edgy, and the thought of attaining the ability to sit in advanced yoga postures like the lotus seemed impossible in my lifetime.

But the edges I felt while sitting on the floor felt like useful ones, and overcoming the other hardships I endured in my life made the temporary discomfort pale in comparison. I decided to make sitting on the floor my new norm in pursuit of greater wellness. If I was sitting cross-legged, I elevated my hips from the floor by placing a block or bolster under my seat so that the stretch in my hips was gentle enough to sustain for long periods of sitting. When attempting to kneel, I would put a folded-up blanket between my thighs and calves to keep my knees at an edge I could handle for a few minutes before cycling back to a posture that was easier for me.

Yoga therapists believe that the healing power of yoga is available to everyone regardless of their health, fitness, or limitations, the only caveat being that the individual must be willing to put in the work necessary to cultivate true change. One must be willing to sit at the edge and teach themselves they are safe to grow by breathing deeply and closely monitoring their sensations. They must collect the courage to recognize the root of their pain, to sit with it, accept it, and seek out tangible ways to address it.

As a yoga therapist, I work with bodies of all shapes and sizes, from athletes and the able-bodied to those with severe handicaps and illnesses. Through this work, I have learned that most people only need a bit more awareness of themselves to realize what they need to do in order to heal. Most people have instincts that pop up in the background encouraging them to make healthy changes, but they ignore them like white noise. Given the space, most of my clients discover what they need without any prescription or coercion, and most often these needs are met through small, simple, incremental changes.

How to Use This Book

If you try on the practices in this book, you will encounter discomfort. Thankfully, you have hidden tools you may have forgotten about to manage discomfort, tools that have always been a part of you but were most likely obscured from your mind somewhere shortly after childhood. This book will offer you a new way to look at discomfort and show how to utilize it for empowerment, growth, and self-healing. Implement the practices in this book gradually, perhaps trying on one or two per week to give yourself a chance to notice the effects. It's vitally important to listen to your body when performing these practices. Your body will always tell you what is safe and what is not, but you must listen closely in order to hear it.

This book is not intended to transform you into a yogi. In fact, I don't consider the practices offered within to be yoga practices. They're *human* practices. Each and every one of us have self-healing instincts pre-programmed into our bodies. The yogis were just the first to systemize these practices. You don't need to memorize yoga systems in order to transform. You just need to reconnect with your instincts—instincts that have been buried under trauma, technology, and societal norms. To benefit from this book you only need an open mind and a willingness to experiment with a new way of living, or, more accurately, an ancient way of living, the way our ancestors lived and the way *pain-free people* all over the world still live today.

In Part One of this book I describe how a modern lifestyle is destroying the health of Western societies. If you find all the historical data and cultural statistics boring, skip ahead to Part Two. There you will begin to learn simple ways to fight back against the effects of modern living. You will learn that by confronting your pain and resolving to do something about it through incremental changes to your lifestyle, it is possible to self-heal.

Parts Two and Three serve as a reference manual for building your practice. I offer my opinion on the "eight essential healing postures" all humans should incorporate into daily living in order to self-heal. Visit www.burnyourchair.com for a library of variations and modifications to these postures for different levels of flexibility, injuries, handicaps, chronic conditions, and other physical limitations. If you have special needs that aren't addressed by these modifications, there are links to help you find a yoga therapist who can better modify the practice to keep you safe.

Who This Book Can Help

When asked, "Who can this book help?" I want to answer with some kind of sweeping statement like, "Anyone, of course!" However, I must point out that the majority of the interventions offered in this book utilize the physical body as the gateway to healing, which may leave individuals with severe handicaps, diseases, and other limitations asking, "What about me? There's no way I'll ever be able to do that." To those of you who feel this way I offer that you remain curious, don't drop this book just yet. As my client, Beverly, who is mostly paralyzed from multiple sclerosis, says, "We all have versions of these practices within us. I just need to find my version of walking every day in order to heal."

As much as possible within this text, I try to offer ideas on how to modify the practices. However, some conditions and limitations are so unique that they deserve the attention of a professional. You will know if your conditions require professional supervision if you experience only pain and frustration each time you practice the interventions in this book, no matter how kind you attempt to be to your body or how many modifications you make to manage your discomfort.

Everyone can benefit from professional guidance when seeking healing; however, there are systematic problems with the way professional healing is offered in the West. It's because we all want a magic pill. We want a magic treatment that immediately resolves our pain with little effort on our end. We want our chiropractor to give us a few quick adjustments that will "fix" us. We want our doctor to order surgery or prescribe medicine that will end our pain. The results we receive don't last long, so we get stuck in a cycle of chronic pain and endless treatments.

If you are seeking a magic pill, this book is not for you. The only way you will receive true healing from the practices in this book is if you are willing to be in the driver's seat on the road to recovery. Any true healer would agree with me. Your physical therapist can put you in a cryocuff and help you stretch each week, but they can't make you keep up with your exercises. Your psychotherapist can listen to you vent and offer their understanding, but they can't stop you from continuing to abuse yourself with toxic thoughts.

In the United States we receive "sick care," not health care. The medical system is designed intentionally to keep us stuck in a pattern of cyclical sickness, ensuring that we are customers for life. Why else would health insurance only pay for conditions after they show up instead of helping to prevent those conditions in the first place?

This book can help anyone who feels disempowered by Western medicine to find healing through their own volition. The pages to follow contain practices of self-care that prevent injuries, address stress, cure disease, and relieve pain. Most importantly, this book offers practices that are completely free and immediately available to most bodies. Just remember that this book does not offer a complete care plan for your unique experience and that its practices should be combined thoughtfully with proper nutrition, adequate exercise, and appropriate medicines in a holistic health care package for maximum benefits.

Some conditions that I think are most notably addressed by the practices in this book are:

- Chronic Pain
- Back Pain and Spinal Health
- Knee, Hip, Foot, and Shoulder Pain
- Depression, Anxiety, Stress, Anger Management, and Mental Illness
- PTSD and Other Trauma-Based Conditions
- Arthritis, Fibromyalgia, Multiple Sclerosis, Parkinson's/Lyme Disease
- Osteoporosis, Osteopenia, and Maintaining Bone Health
- Chronic Fatigue, Adrenal Fatigue, Lack of Focus/Motivation
- Sleeplessness and Restlessness
- Obesity and Overweight, Eating Disorders, Diabetes
- Cardiovascular Disease and Heart Health
- Respiratory Health
- Balance, Fall Prevention, and Healthy Aging
- Hyper/Hypothyroidism and Other Endocrine Disorders
- Athletics and Human Performance
- Pregnancy, Childbirth, and Raising Children

Evidence

The list above is bold to say the least. I would not make these claims if there weren't evidence to back them up. Whenever possible, the practices offered in this book are presented with relevant scientific studies. You'll find in-text citations following both direct quotes and paraphrased material as superscript numbers. These numbers match references in the back of the book.

Phrases such as "evidence suggests" or "research indicates" invite you to remain curious. New studies are being conducted every day, the results of which can contradict everything we thought we knew. The practices offered in this book do not require you to accept the science presented as absolute truth. Rather, they ask for your curious experimentation. Try on the practices while listening to the wisdom of your body. Your body will tell you whether or not the scientific evidence resonates with your unique experience.

If you're feeling extra curious or even a bit skeptical, visit the original source. Most of the research presented in this book was found free on the internet via databases like Google Scholar. Utilize them to form your own opinions about the validity of each practice offered. Remember, the real research is to be done in *your* lab, *in your body.* That is the kind of research that will bring about true healing.

Illustrations

Throughout this book you will find line drawings of people assuming *active rest postures*—instinctive human postures that optimize the health of the human body. These healing shapes are shown in contrast with examples of painful *learned postures* that wreak havoc on our health. Each image is accompanied by a caption that links it to the text which summarizes the points being referenced. Skimming through the book to browse the illustrations and read a few captions is a great way to obtain a bird's-eye view of the practices offered within the book.

The illustrations were designed to inspire you to find variations of healing shapes that work for your unique body. Unlike other posture modification techniques, the *Burn Your Chair* method focuses on one's sense of self—not strict rules about alignment—for determining whether a position is safe for that individual. While there are alignment cues offered in the text, they are not hard-and-fast rules. No one can tell you exactly what these positions should "look like" when performed by your unique body other than your body itself. It's far more important to pay attention to how the practices feel rather than how they look.

All of the images in this book are an artist's rendition of ***real people*** demonstrating the postures. People of all ages, shapes, sizes, and levels of health and fitness were recruited to be models for the illustrations. The intention behind this diversity is to show that healing shapes are available (in some variation) in most bodies. When attempting a new practice from this book, it's not safe (nor useful) to try to force yourself to look like the people in the pictures. These are members of your human family, but they are not you. In a similar position, you could look a bit alike, but you will always be you, and therefore your experience will always be unique. Looking at the images with empathy instead of comparison invites you to treat yourself in a similar fashion. Using the images in this way will keep your body safe and ensure that your practice is fruitful.

The ink master behind the images in this book is my longtime friend Kristen Jussila. When asked to comment on her experience of illustrating the book, Kristen had this to say:

> *Creating the images for this book changed the way I move and rest. As the images came to life, depicting people of all shapes and sizes moving to improve their well being, I was reminded to focus on my own. Through our collaboration together, Ari helped me unearth inherent knowledge that was buried deep within me. By reshaping how I moved and held my body, I realized that as a child I was practicing these healing behaviors instinctively. I only needed a gentle reminder to realize that my body knew what was best. It was an honor being a part of this project because it truly lightened my life. I hope that Ari's words and my illustrations inspire others on their own healing journey.*

To find more visual references for the practices offered in this book, visit the *Burn Your Chair* bonus resource guide at *www.burnyourchair.com*.

PART ONE

Discovering the Roots
of Our Pain

From an evolutionary perspective, the human body was designed for movement. Our ancestors moved a lot, and when they weren't moving, they were
arranging themselves in active rest postures. The combination of these two
practices kept the body supple and strong and the mind alert and engaged.
Over the past century, most of us living modern lives have decreased or
eliminated completely our time spent in these practices. As a result, we are
constantly sick, in pain, and we die younger. The proliferation of technology over the past few decades has made the problem much worse. We are
beginning to devolve into chronic pain and disease. However, not all hope
is lost. The solution is as simple as reconnecting with our roots and combining the abilities of our ancestors with the advantages of technological
evolution.

1

Is Sitting Really "the New Smoking"?

"Sitting is more dangerous than smoking, kills more people than HIV, and is more treacherous than para-chuting. We are sitting ourselves to death."
—Dr. James Levine

Compared to our parents and grandparents, we spend more and more time in environments that limit our ability to move and promote prolonged periods of inactivity. Our jobs, schools, cars, and homes are all designed around one fundamental position: sitting. The result is that people move less and sit more. From an evolutionary perspective, humans were designed for movement. Work, play, and rest should involve various anatomical positions such as squatting, kneeling, and hanging from an overhead grip as well as complex movement patterns that connect the positions together. In fact, anthropologists have determined that human beings are capable of *at least* 1,000 body positions.[1]

Children of the 21st century may not live as long as their parents due to trends in heart disease, diabetes, addiction, certain types of cancer, and other lifestyle-based diseases.[2] This isn't exactly groundbreaking science. We've known for decades the dangers of being inactive. The seminal study of the differences between prolonged sitting and moving regularly took place in Britain in 1953. Dr. Jerry Morris demonstrated that conductors who walked up and down the aisles on double-decker buses all day had significantly lower rates of early death caused by heart disease compared to the drivers sitting at the front of the bus.[3] This said a lot to the medical community about the benefits of regular exercise. Only recently have researchers come back to reexamine the negative effects of sedentary behavior.

It's important to know the difference between being physically inactive and being sedentary. The World Health Organization suggests that adults engage in at least 150 minutes of moderate physical activity each week in order to optimize health.[4] You are considered *physically inactive* if you do not meet this minimum. This doesn't necessarily mean, however, that you spend long periods of time sitting, reclining, or lying down on furniture, which are considered *sedentary behaviors*. For example, if you are a cashier and you work on your feet all day without ever increasing your heart rate or challenging your muscles, and you don't have a hobby that offers you those demands, you are considered physically inactive (but not necessarily sedentary). However, if you decide to sit in a chair all day to make checking people out easier on your aching feet, you are taking the gentle demands of your job away and engaging in sedentary behavior.

Combining physical inactivity with prolonged sedentary behavior can be deadly. Moreover, the increased risk of premature death associated with sedentary

Remaining seated for the majority of the day correlates with chronic pain, disease, and early death, whereas maintaining a baseline of gentle activity throughout the day protects our physical and mental health.

18

living is unaffected by your level of physical activity.[5] Simply put, you can't exercise away the effects of being sedentary. Long periods of sitting cause poor use of blood sugar, weakening and shortening of muscles, increased blood pressure, elevated blood cholesterol, warped posture, and raise the risk of premature death. The high prevalence of back pain in Western societies is most certainly related to our recent increase in time spent sitting. Higher amounts of daily sitting correlate with weight gain as well as an increased risk of diabetes and heart disease, even in people who exercise regularly. The National Cancer Institute warns that sedentary living increases an individual's chances of developing certain types of cancer, regardless of their level of physical activity.[6]

Research indicates that long periods of sitting cause depression. A prolonged sedentary lifestyle may increase the risk of developing mental health disorders or exacerbate existing ones. These findings are particularly relevant to Western societies; in the United States alone we have seen a 33 percent increase in the annual suicide rate from 1999 to 2017, the highest it has been since World War II.[7] An increase that one could posit directly correlates to a similar increase in sedentary living.

Correlates like these are a large part of my taking a stand against sedentary living because I lost my father to suicide. Many of my family members suffer from debilitating mental illness. They all have one thing in common: at their happiest and highest functioning, they lived lives that involved consistent activity. As their levels of activity decreased and their time spent sedentary increased, a noticeable decline in their mental health soon followed.

Given our better understanding of sedentary behavior, health professionals are calling sitting "the new smoking," comparing the sitting epidemic of our time to the smoking epidemic of the 20th century. So if "sitting is the new smoking," how do we quit?

The Practice of Active Rest

Engaging in manual labor throughout the day used to be our way of life. Hunting, foraging, cooking, building—our survival as a species hinged on completion of physical activities that are now considered hobbies. Advances in agriculture, manufacturing, and industry have made many of these skills obsolete in modern life. Additionally, our society, economy, and environment are continuously being reengineered to make life more convenient and therefore more sedentary.

However, emerging evidence now indicates that living a predominantly sedentary lifestyle *does not* necessarily cause poor health. Scientists are studying cultures around the world that do not share our propensity for pain and disease. It's not at all surprising that people of these cultures easily meet the weekly guidelines for physical activity. Yet shockingly, they also spend as much time sedentary as we do! How can this be? Researchers theorize that it doesn't matter whether we are sedentary or not. The problem lies in how we choose to behave while sedentary. We either select sedentary activities that keep the body partially active, or we completely disengage in a way that gradually degrades our health.[8]

Healthy rest is being taken away from us. The chair and its many variations have removed the need for natural human resting postures which keep the body strong and supple. These positions promote a consistent baseline of muscular activity that protects our health. Instead we rely on artificial support, disengaging completely and allowing the design of foreign objects to deform our bodies into painful shapes that over time become permanently ingrained.

Maintaining healthy posture through self-awareness in order to encourage restoration of energy is what I call *active rest*. Active rest is the type of rest that we partake in while awake and engaged. It promotes regeneration of body tissues through gentle stretching and gradual strengthening. It improves circulation, promotes relaxation, and develops greater body awareness and self-control. When we perform active resting postures, our body is empowered by the ergonomic shape.

The self-awareness needed for engaging in active rest also alerts us when we have been in one shape for too long. This leads to the practice of *posture cycling,* changing shape intermittently to meet the demands of the moment and the signals of the body. Periodic posture cycling ensures that the body is not exposed to one stressor for too long. It allows us to find shapes that better assist us in the task at hand rather than remaining in one position for everything we do.

1. Is Sitting Really "the New Smoking"?

Contrast is the spice of life. When we jump into a cool pool of water after baking for hours in the summer sun, the contrast of sensations makes us feel alive. Staying in one extreme or the other for too long is unsafe, as it will inevitably cause us pain or disease. The contrast found in posture cycling is a vital component of what makes active rest so useful in an age dominated by a single shape. You will learn more about active rest postures and ways to cycle through them later in the book. For more variations of these practices, check out the bonus resource guide at *www.burnyourchair.com*.

The more you practice active rest postures, the more your body begins to associate them with a sense of well-being. Once your body is trained to recognize certain postures as cues to relax, relaxation happens automatically upon revisiting them. Combining active rest with mindful breathing trains our nervous system over time to maintain balance between the stress and relaxation responses. This makes active rest a cumulative practice; the more you do it, the better you feel. Active rest postures are *innate*. Your body is pre-programmed with them. When given the proper encouragement, the right environment, and the freedom to do so, you will naturally move into them.

To benefit from these ancient human resting postures you must reconnect with primordial human instincts. You can see these instincts demonstrated by a developing child, who will assume the postures outlined in this book without being taught to do so as they explore their growing body. These postures are invaluable to our health compared to *learned postures,* the habitual shapes we mimic from the unhealthy modeling of others or from when we rely on artificial support. Our bodies are so good at adapting to whatever we expose them to that although learned postures cause us pain, they eventually become ingrained. Stuck in these shapes we suffer a cycle of lethargy, depression, pain, and a myriad of other symptoms. We forget our bodies are capable of so much more.

An example of a learned posture is what I like to call the "too-cool-for-school slump." We all know this shape: head hanging forward, slouched shoulders, rounded back and tucked tailbone. A slump like this weakens our neck, back, and core muscles, compresses our shoulders, glutes, hamstrings, and vertebral discs. The primary reason we fall into this shape is that in the moment it feels like we are conserving energy. While slumping may require less mental energy, it limits other bodily functions such as breathing and digestion which actively generate new energy.

Passive rest is resting with a disengaged body and mind. We do need this kind of rest in our daily lives. In small doses, it can be very healing. Passive rest is useful when we don't need to protect our body through posture. It gives us a much needed break when our body has reached its limit and active rest is no longer possible. Examples of healthy passive rest are short bouts of chair sitting, lying down on furniture, swinging in a hammock, or soaking in a

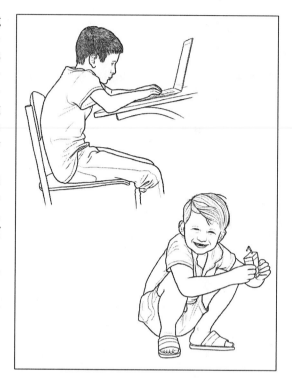

Instinctive positions like the squat are replaced by chairs in modern societies. Conforming to the chair shape for long periods leaves us stuck in painful posture. Learned postures like this diminish the capabilities of our bodies and lead to a life stifled by chronic pain and disease.

hot tub. The key here is that the exposure is brief so that it balances out the active parts of life but does not become excessive. Spending hours reclining in front of a screen does not meet this criteria. Passive rest performed for long periods of time in unhealthy shapes is a large part of why a modern lifestyle leads to chronic pain.

The average American adult now spends upwards of six and a half hours per day sitting, an increase of about an hour per day since 2007. For teens the numbers are even worse, climbing to upwards of eight hours per day.[9] Television used to be public enemy number one when the obesity epidemic was the main target of anti-sitting crusades, but time spent watching TV seems to be remaining steady as sit times increase. Computer and personal device usage are on the uprise, and as these new culprits get smaller and smaller, we find ourselves leaning in further and further towards their gravitational pull, a pull so powerful that new learned postures are being created, such as the physically debilitating and emotionally destructive shape known affectionately as "tech neck."

In indigenous cultures around the world, it is not common to sit in chairs for long periods of time. Ailments such as back pain are almost nonexistent, even though these people spend significantly more hours doing hard physical labor than we do. These people must maintain healthy levels of physical activity, eat what the land provides, and regularly assume active rest postures rather than sit in chairs. Their behavior is driven by survival and environmental necessity, not societal norms. Furniture is too heavy to migrate with, and resources are better used for hunting and gathering. Unfortunately, indigenous populations such as those in the United States, Canada, and Australia have lost these practices due to modernization. They suffer worse than we do from the trappings of lifestyle-based death and disease due to the destruction of their culture and systematic marginalization.

Indigenous people like the Gadaba of Eastern India assume active rest postures to meet the needs of daily life. People in societies such as these report significantly lower levels of chronic pain than we do and do not share our biomarkers for heart disease and cancer.

Part One—Discovering the Roots of Our Pain

Back pain specialist Esther Gokhale (author of *8 Steps to a Pain-free Back*) traveled the world studying the habits of indigenous people to seek out the common bond that affords them a life free from pain. These societies known for their hard physical work ethic and their lack of chronic pain could be dubbed ***pain-free societies***. Gokhale interviewed, took photos of and videotaped people who spent most of their day walking with water buckets on their heads, collecting firewood, or sitting on the ground weaving baskets. "I have a picture of these two women who spend seven to nine hours a day bent over gathering water chestnuts," she says. "They're quite old. But the truth is: they don't have any back pain."

When confronted with this new idea, "sitting is the new smoking," Gokhale vehemently disagrees, stating, "we are much better designed than that." Gokhale posits that the painful consequences that come from long periods of inactivity cannot be blamed entirely on sitting; poor posture is the real culprit of our chronic pain. She believes it has become fashionable to slump because our society finds aloof and carefree shapes more attractive than healthy posture. In my malleable prepubescent years I picked up this slumpy shape from the cool kids in the neighborhood. I have a distinct memory of my friend's older brother sitting on a curb with a group of girls, crumpled over in the cool kid slump, smoking a cigarette. Just like that I was both a smoker and a sloucher. As an adult concerned with my own well-being, I've kicked the smokes. Contrary to what one might think, it has been much harder to remove the slump from my physical vocabulary. To this day I still have to constantly fight the urge to sit disengaged in an unattractive and pain-inducing "C" shape.

I can't blame my battle with poor posture entirely on the cool kids. Thinking back to the shape of the triangular plastic desk chairs I grew up sitting in at school, I realize that this was the only shape made available to me. These torture devices encourage the tail-tucked shape, sacrificing ergonomics for casual comfort. If we compare these types of chairs to the more minimalist wooden desk chairs found in an old one-room schoolhouse, we see the latter only supports the mid-back, leaving room for the pelvis and shoulders to be rolled back in a healthy position. This version of seated posture encourages physical and mental engagement. Looking beyond our education system, we see similar disfiguring trends in the design of modern furniture.

Living a Life Free from Pain

I missed out on so much before discovering the healing power of active rest. For years as a young adult I was plagued by chronic pain brought on from hours of sitting slumped over in front of screens. I avoided long road trips with friends because of back pain I couldn't explain. Unbeknownst to me, I was driving with my tail tucked between my legs. It was as if my hips and back were glued together. I had no awareness that this part of my body was under my control or that the body shapes I chose were the protagonists for my constant pain.

In the years to follow I discovered yoga and other forms of ***therapeutic exercise,*** movements that improve mobility and strength, reduce pain, prevent injury, and create a bridge between the body and mind. Other examples of therapeutic exercise include dance, calisthenics, weightlifting, swimming, and rock climbing. Any type of exercise that encourages us to be more mindful of our bodies, provides opportunities for healthy physical shifts, and offers emotional catharsis could be considered therapeutic. It doesn't matter the modality of movement; rather it's the initial intention of the practitioner that makes therapeutic exercise unique from exercise styles which treat the muscles as if they were separate from the mind. This is why the coaches and trainers who actually help people change are the ones who context each workout with the goals their clients are reaching for instead of offering each client cookie-cutter exercise programs.

If you plan to begin exercising more regularly and hope to receive therapeutic benefits, you are much more likely to succeed if you set an intention for your practice and enter each workout with that intention in mind. For instance, if your intention is to use exercise to treat depression, you should consider modes of exercise that easily release the body's natural antidepressants, such as jogging or cycling. Each time you exercise, you should remain aware of the original intention of empowering yourself through the movements. If instead your primary reason for exercising is to prevent or rehabilitate injuries, simple bodyweight exercises performed consistently should meet your needs. Finding the right therapeutic exercise for achieving your own transformation is a process. You must experiment over the course of your life to find the mode of exercise most therapeutic to you, knowing that it will change as your body and life circumstances change. Regardless of how you move, if you discover a passion for what you are doing, you'll keep coming back to the practice again and again. This is the type of consistency that has the power to change your life and end your pain.

Although martial arts played a role in creating my pain and injuries, it also gave me a reason to take care of myself. To be a better martial artist I needed to do more than just drill the techniques. I needed to eat better, stretch, and get enough rest so that I could train to my full potential. Martial arts brought me closer to homeostasis and started me on a path towards self-mastery. It provided me with therapeutic benefits that gradually accumulated and culminated in my transformation. Combining your favorite forms of therapeutic exercise with the practice of active rest is an excellent strategy for achieving a healthy balance of strength, flexibility, and hardiness that are essential for cultivating a pain-free life.

I use the term "pain-free" a lot in this book. "But pain is an inevitable part of our lives, how can we prevent it entirely?" *Living a life free from pain* means you realize your conscious control over the pain in your life so that it never becomes a prison for your body and mind. This does not mean that you never experience pain. It means that when you experience pain, you know you have tools to cope, and you use them. Your body is amazing. It contains the miraculous ability to self-heal. If you want to live a life free from pain, you must believe in this ability and encourage it every day. Beyond the wonders of the body, you contain an additional safeguard against the prison of chronic pain: your mind. You have the mental capability to overcome any physical pain you will ever experience. If you remain steadfast in believing these truths, you too can live a life free from pain.

A pain-free life starts with a collection of self-healing tools. You can easily find the tools offered in this book by looking for the word **practice** in bold letters. Practices like therapeutic exercise and active rest allow us to "work with our pain." Working like this helps us cultivate an attitude of, "Yes, I can. I can heal my body. I can overcome pain." The first tool I offer you is the practice of pelvic tilting. The pelvic tilt exercise helps us reestablish conscious control over our pelvic alignment. Proper pelvic alignment is **the foundation for healthy posture**. This makes the pelvic tilt exercise an invaluable tool in working towards a pain-free life. With consistent practice, the foundation for healthy posture can once again become an instinctive place you return to in response to pain.

Practice—Pelvic Tilts

1. To practice proper pelvic alignment imagine your pelvis as a bucket. When you find yourself in a slump, tip the front of your hips forward as if you were pouring water out of the bucket in front of you. Squeeze your glutes and tighten your core muscles to stabilize. This will slightly arch your low back and create a foundation for your upper back to lengthen.
2. To make this a repeatable exercise, lie down on the ground and alternate between a posterior pelvic tilt and an anterior pelvic tilt. First, push your low back flat to the floor by squeezing your core and glutes, pouring water from the back of the bucket. This is a posterior pelvic tilt.
3. Next, relax your core and glutes as you press your tailbone down and allow your low back to arch, pouring water from the front of the bucket. This is an anterior pelvic tilt. Creating awareness of your hip position is the key. Recall the bucket image as you roll from posterior to anterior.
4. Once you are comfortable with the two extremes, come to a seated or standing position and seek neutral alignment. Again, with the bucket analog, try not to spill any water from the front or back of your bucket. When standing and walking, avoid spilling water out the sides of the bucket by dropping one hip more than the other. Engage your core muscles and glutes to stabilize the bucket.

Maintaining healthy pelvic alignment throughout our day requires mental alertness and muscular engagement, which is why we find it fatiguing. With practice the self-awareness required by active rest gradually becomes our norm. We then feel more alert and energized in the active seat and active standing positions. This self-awareness eventually becomes an internal diagnostic tool that is constantly running in the background of our mind, alerting us when it detects that our body is in compromising positions and prompting us to adjust to prevent future problems.

Through therapeutic exercises like pelvic tilts combined with stretching, I was able to unglue my hips from my back and reestablish a mental connection to this part of the body. This rebuilt my foundation for healthy posture. Soon after implementing this practice I noticed sitting was more comfortable and required less effort. Everything I did from a seat came with more ease and greater attention. I wasn't being pulled away from my desk by my aching back. I could stay in meditation longer with less pain. I noticed a sense of levity in my yoga practice and increased agility in athletics. My posture changed so drastically that when I would run into old friends, they would ask me things like, "Did you get taller?" and "What's your secret?" Even strangers were more likely to strike up a conversation or ask me for help as my posture communicated that I was kind, capable, and open rather than uncomfortable, awkward, and potentially dangerous.

Practicing proper pelvic alignment the rest of my body felt bigger and lighter. It encouraged the rest of my body to adjust into healthy alignment. Untucking my tail allowed me to stack my spine and roll my shoulders back which brought my entire body into a more ergonomic and pain-free shape. Utilizing self-awareness to detect the source of our pain and adjust the body accordingly is what I call **biofeedback.** This is not to be confused with modern "biofeedback therapy" in which computer sensors read muscle activity, heart rate, and perspiration, displaying it to patients so that they can visually recognize tension and do relaxation exercises in response. Rather than relying on technology, you can create this same self-awareness by focusing on your position and noticing how changing it affects you. A simple biofeedback exercise is to pull your shoulder blades together in response to upper back pain. As you do so, notice how your shoulders are pulled back, your chest is widened and your chin lifts up. Just as you did with the pelvic tilt exercise, shift back and forth. Alternate between squeezing the shoulder blades together and letting them go slack. Try holding the squeeze while breathing deeply. Notice the ease and fullness of your breath in this shape compared to how your breath feels in the deactivated shape. Practicing biofeedback will reeducate your body in regards to which positions cause pain and how to adjust to relieve it. For more examples of therapeutic biofeedback exercises, check out the bonus resource guide at *www.burnyourchair.com.*

Sitting actively requires our attention and effort, of which many of us feel we have none left to spare. This is why, over time, members of Western societies are losing their ability to assume valuable healing postures innate to the human body. We are much more interested in short-term comfort than we are in long-term wellness. By relying on artificial support, we are erasing our ***kinesthetic traditions***, the postures and movements passed down from generation to generation. Much like language, these physical traditions pass on important information about communal health. Instead of taking the time to teach our children how to move safely and maintain healthy posture, we strap them into car seats and hypnotize them with screens.

Innate postures that we may have lost can become available to us again. Sitting or standing with a new foundation created by proper

Kinesthetic traditions like maintaining healthy posture are being erased by technology and societal norms. If we wish to improve communal health, we must reinstate these traditions. The health of our family starts at home.

29

pelvic alignment allows our vertebrae to stack on top of each other. This utilizes the intelligent design of our spine, decreasing the effort necessary for holding ourselves erect. Combined with core engagement, mindfully stacked posture creates gentle spinal traction, and separation of the spinal tissues. This separation allows spinal muscles to lengthen and relax and decompresses the vertebral discs. When space is created within joints in this way, hydration flows in to heal and protect the tissues. With healthy spinal alignment, our other joints and tissues align, improving circulation and the flow of breath.

This is not to say that you must always have perfect posture or never sit in a plush chair. Even if you must sit for long periods of time due to work, injuries, or other limitations, you don't have to fall victim to the pathologies of sedentary living. I theorize instead that the higher level of awareness that comes from the mind-body connection I have described allows us to protect our body through self-preservation instincts. The combination of biofeedback, thoughtful cycling through active rest postures, and regular therapeutic exercise can keep us well aligned and protect our mental health regardless of our circumstances.

Over time the effects of these three practices—biofeedback, posture cycling, and therapeutic exercise—accumulate into long-term wellness. These aren't separate ideas to be inserted into life randomly. Rather, they are lifestyle choices that must be consistently practiced together to be most effective. It is a distinctly Western practice to be lost in painful inactivity during our workday and then seek to reverse its effects with a brief bout of exercise. This method of destressing is ineffective in combating the woes of sedentary living. In fact, it may be quite dangerous to care for ourselves in this way. We can't fight off the effects of eight hours of poor posture with one hour of activity, even if the exercise mode is therapeutic. Our bodies just don't work that way.

What we can do instead is create a higher baseline of awareness in our bodies. This way we maintain the type of posture that protects us from stagnation and recharges us in preparation for more vigorous activities. The practice of active rest can help us to create a more engaged version of our bodies and minds when we are at work and a more fully disengaged version of ourselves when winding down for bed. By practicing consistently, we begin to gain agency over the contrast of work and rest in our lives.

2

Returning to Our Roots

"We are marvelously designed creatures. We have inherent grace and strength, like every other creature on the planet. We have evolved to sit, walk, run, jump, climb, carry, and even dance without pain. If we respect our natural design, our bodies heal spontaneously, and we can function well for close to a century. Indeed, there are many populations where most people live painlessly into old age."
—Esther Gokhale

The human body has the miraculous power to spontaneously self-heal. For many injuries, diseases, and conditions, the most effective treatment is rest. We could say that rest is the key to healing. But rest in the West has devolved under the influence of technology so that it no longer resembles our ancestors' rest habits, which allowed them to overcome illness and injury without medicine or surgery.

Our up-and-at-'em society tells us that if we go to bed early, we might miss something important, that if we lay down on the ground to watch the clouds pass by, life will be passing us by as well. The emphasis placed on work over rest in modern society has disturbed our relationship with healthy resting practices This has left modern humans seemingly incapable of rest. We must change the way we view rest in order to encourage healthy rest habits to become a societal norm in order to improve communal health. Rest is the wellspring from which all energy is derived, not a practice only for the self-indulgent or lazy. Rest should be seen as the number one ingredient necessary for maximizing the experience of living within the human body. In order to escape the chronic diseases associated with a modern lifestyle, rest must become guilt-free.

Part One—Discovering the Roots of Our Pain

There was a time when rest came much easier to us. If you were brought up in a safe and loving home, chances are someone worked very hard to create the best conditions for you to receive adequate rest. Smart parents gradually ease their children into independence with their resting habits, putting limits on screen time as well as stimulating food and drink, and instituting a lights-out rule. Why then as adults don't we protect and encourage rest in our own lives in a similar way? It seems that once there is no one helping us to maintain our healthy rest habits, we fall prey to cultural conditioning that destroys the relationship with rest our parents attempted to create for us.

I define *rest* as the process of internal upkeep and energy creation within the body that is facilitated by stillness and relaxation. By slowing oneself physically and using tools such as mindful breathing to downregulate the body's systems, we can recoup our strength and refresh our mind. Waking rest can be found in meditation or anything that has a meditative effect. Some examples of restful waking activities are reading, writing, making music, singing, bathing, hobbying, and observing nature. Even certain types of movement could be considered restful practices, as they create more energy than they consume, such as tai chi, mindful walking, or restorative yoga.

The condition of being chronically under rested is surely an affliction unique to modern man and is likely related to our propensity for chronic pain. Human beings are animals. Animals are a part of nature. When an animal is sick or hurt, it doesn't look for medicine or even search for food. It simply finds a safe place to rest and dedicates all of its time to letting the body heal naturally. Therefore, the easiest way to heal our self-inflicted hurt is by encouraging the natural healing capability of our bodies. We can do this by reintroducing the practices of our ancestors into our daily lives.

Following the circadian rhythm is one of the easiest ways to improve our relationship with rest. It's very simple: Sleep when it's dark, and wake with the sun. As hunter-gatherers we had no other way of operating since following the sun was a matter of life or death unless the moon was full. Before the invention of electric light, farmers couldn't operate without the sun, so waking at sunrise and winding down at sunset was the only option. As light bulbs have become smaller and more powerful, it has become almost impossible to escape the light. We have to intentionally shut it out or turn it off. It's not just the lights in our rooms; the screens we stare at after the sun has gone down trick our bodies into believing the sun is still out and that we should stay awake to take advantage.

If instead we cooperate with nature by powering down our devices and turning the lights down low as the sun goes down, we reunite with the flow of the cosmos and reestablish our own internal rhythm. The less humans fight the night through artificial light, the less electricity is consumed, and in turn fewer fossil fuels are burned. Other examples of ancient human practices that optimize our health and the health of the planet are eating a plant-based diet, engaging in biodiverse farming, walking more and driving less. Our bodies are wonderful microcosmic examples of how to encourage the healing processes innate in nature. By restoring the natural rhythms of life, we get the most out of life while also allowing our planet to thrive and nurture living things as it has for millions of years.

I call the practice of behaving more like our ancestors in order to maximize our health **returning to our roots.** There are many other ways in which we can emulate our ancestors in order to maximize our quality of life. In fact, there are cultures all over the world who are demonstrating this, cultures who never lost these practices and still live following the flow of nature, thriving at the peak of human potential.

Primal Posture

World-renowned back pain specialist and acupuncturist to the stars, Esther Gokhale, had a self-healing journey similar to mine. After giving birth to her first child, she was diagnosed as having a herniated disc and underwent the prescribed surgery seeking relief. After only a year, the pain returned. Her doctors advised another surgery, but this time Gokhale refused. She had grown weary of Western medicine repeatedly failing to give her a life free from pain. She felt that the treatments she was offered by her doctors only covered up the problem rather than solved the underlying issues. This time, Gokhale wanted a permanent fix:

Part One—Discovering the Roots of Our Pain

I learned about L'Institut d'Aplomb in Paris, France, where Noelle Perez teaches an anthropologically-based posture modification technique. Her theory is that we in industrialized countries don't use our bodies well, that this misuse can cause pain and damage, and that we have to learn from people in traditional cultures. The theory resonated with my childhood memories of growing up in India. I remembered listening to my Dutch mother marvel at how gracefully our Indian maid went about her duties and how easily the laborers in the street carried their burdens.[1]

While studying under Noelle Perez, Gokhale researched other physiotherapies. The Alexander Technique and The Feldenkrais Method posture modification protocols provided her with more pain relief and offered more evidence that validated her childhood memories.

She theorized that in cultures where these postures were not lost traditions, people must be free from pain.

Over the course of the next decade, Gokhale traveled to remote parts of the planet to observe people who live isolated from the influence of modern life. She went to mountain settlements in Ecuador, remote fishing villages in Portugal, and tiny towns in Western Africa. As she photographed natives and locals, she noticed a trend in how they held themselves. A regal posture that she found quite compelling: Pelvis tipped forward, glutes engaged when standing,

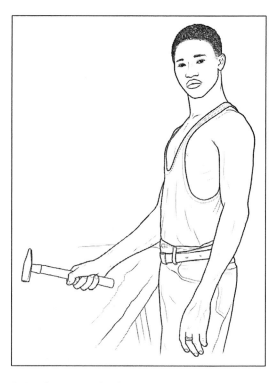

Pain-free people demonstrate a regal shape that back pain specialist Esther Gokhale refers to as "primal posture." Gokhale believes this active posture is the key to their pain-free lives.

34

an even spinal groove, shoulders behind the torso, and a long neck with the chin slightly tipped forward—a shape Gokhale refers to as "primal posture." She interviewed these regal individuals to get a sense of the effects of pain in their lives, but as she had predicted, most had no pain to report.

The people she interviewed focused most of their daily energy on a few repetitive tasks that ranged from sedentary to vigorous in demand. Yet regardless of their level of physical activity, there were no differences in reported pain. Chores that we would consider "back-breaking labor" weren't causing them the same problems they cause us, but neither were long-term sedentary tasks like sitting on the ground weaving baskets all day. Tasks ranging from carrying heavy loads long distances on their heads, bending over repeatedly to gather up fishing nets, or squatting to gather water chestnuts all day didn't seem to affect them negatively. This suggests that chronic pain is not solved by avoiding sedentary behavior nor by striving to be constantly physically active, that there is something more to how modern cultures conduct both sedentary and active tasks that puts them at risk when compared to pain-free societies.

Gokhale compared the photographs she took of pain-free societies with pictures of people from Western societies taken over the past two centuries. Primal posture could still be seen in Western bodies at the turn of the 20th century. However, starting in the 1920s, Gokhale noted, "it became fashionable to slouch." When posing for pictures, entertainers could be seen thrusting their pelvises and necks forward in unhealthy alignment. And just like that, the cool kid slump was born, and with it a cultural propensity towards chronic pain began to arise as well.

Gokhale continued to dig. She studied old anatomical texts to see if there was a correlation between this shift in culturally influenced posture and the structure of the human body. When comparing an anatomy book published in 1911 with one published in 1990, she discovered a shocking phenomenon. The spine considered to be normal in 1911 had gentle spinal curves that created a J-shape, whereas a spine considered to be normal in 1990 had accentuated curves that created the S-shape we are told today is healthy. The lumbar (low back) curve was most notably changed, and Gokhale posits this is where much of modern back pain comes from. The exaggeration of this curve puts uneven pressure on the lower vertebral discs and discourages proper pelvic alignment. She was able to find examples of the J-shaped spine all throughout history in drawings from Leonardo DaVinci, ancient Greek statues, and religious idols in Thailand but could find no evidence of the S-shaped spine anywhere but in modern texts.

Gokhale concluded that there must have been a disconnect in the way we pass down kinesthetic traditions from one generation to the next that caused this postural shift and changed the shape of our spine. "In industrialized societies, many families have become geographically dispersed, with couples raising their children far away from parents and grandparents." This spreading out of families coincided with the advent of the automobile, which also became widely used around the 1920s and would eventually become another daily seat from which our naturally healthy posture would deform.

Without grandparents showing parents how to properly nurse or carry their children, there became an immediate disconnect from ancient kinesthetic traditions at birth. Children are born with instincts that drive them to utilize the design of their bodies in a way that is pain-free and ergonomic (discussed later in greater detail). But in these formative years, children are always watching

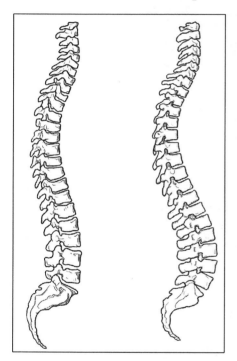

Notice the subtle differences between an artist's rendition of a healthy spine found in an anatomical text from 1911 (left) and one found in an anatomical text from 1990 (right). Notice the gentle curves of the spine on the left and the exaggerated curves of the spine on the right. Exaggerated spinal curvature may be a piece of the chronic pain puzzle plaguing our people.

us and mimicking our every move, and unfortunately, healthy human instincts can be erased by poor modeling. If we hope to defeat the chronic pain epidemic before it can affect the next generation, we need to begin studying, practicing, and passing down the kinesthetic traditions of cultures where pain isn't present, so our children can live lives free from pain.

Ancient Kinesthetic Wisdom

Other than a regal standing posture, what do these indigenous and traditional cultures with little to no pain have in common? Besides having more natural diets and spending more of their day moving, scientists note that they work and rest in active, ergonomic positions—positions that many in the West have lost due to decades of relying on the artificial support of chairs. Pain-free societies utilize these positions out of convenience for meeting the logistical needs of manual labor and tasks of daily living. Unsupported by elaborate tools or infrastructure, their instincts inspire them

Children are born with healthy instincts for developing and maintaining good posture. However, if we discourage these instincts by strapping them to booster seats and baby buckets, their bodies are forced to adapt. This sets them up for a life plagued by pain, disease and dysfunction.

to operate the body in a way that is safe and mindful. This practice creates a higher baseline of physical activity and mental awareness in their bodies, which may be the key to their pain-free lives. Whether they are fishermen who are standing, squatting, and bending over for most of the day or basket weavers who are sitting on the ground all day, pain-free people arrange their bodies in ways that save energy and prevent injury.

These people are more in tune with their bodies because their lives depend on it. There's no workman's comp or unemployment insurance protecting their livelihood if they're careless and perform a movement with poor posture. Their work environments are either the great outdoors or minimalistic shelters with sit-stand workstations. They're unlikely to ride in a car or sit in a chair for much of their day. When they do sit, their seats are firm and supportive and not especially cushy or "comfortable." Living in more natural environments and working within minimal infrastructure forces them to maintain their primal posture throughout the day so that they can get the most out of their bodies. When their workday is over, they decompress from their physical efforts through active rest. Without furniture to flop down on or screens to stare at, they stay in tune with their bodies as they go about nightly routines. They flow through different positions as they tend to their camp, prepare and share meals, and get ready to sleep. The ancient shapes they make during their nightly routine were modeled to them as healthy and proper by their parents and grandparents.

In the 1930s, behavioral scientists at Yale's Institute of Human Relations started to develop a collection of research materials to promote understanding of cultural diversity and commonality in the past and present. One product of this project was eHRAF, a digital database of anthropological and archaeological studies of world cultures. This database has made it easier to examine topical information from many sources. In her groundbreaking article, "A Cross Cultural Look at Posture in eHRAF," Dr. Francine Barone analyzes the reports of anthropologists who studied pain-free people all over the world in relation to their posture and rest habits. Dr. Barone highlights the concept of posture cycling by citing an anthropologist as he describes the habits of the Bedouin, a nomadic tribe of the Middle East and Africa:

2. Returning to Our Roots

When a man is narrating a story, he sits on his crossed legs.... During a meal he kneels on his left knee and sits on his left heel ... while inspecting anything or testing a weapon, he kneels on both knees and sits on his heels ... when he washes his hands, he squats.... When it is hot, he lies down on his stomach ... when he takes a nap ... he turns over on his back....[2]

More than half of the postures mentioned above are replaced by artificial seats in our modern life. We must relearn these shapes in order to escape our pain.

Once you begin weaving the healing postures outlined in this book into your daily life, posture cycling will be a key part of your practice. Much like a roast on a spit, we want our bodies to be gently exposed to the pressures of gravity and tension, gradually warming around the edges all day. It isn't that sitting in chairs should be avoided completely; rather sitting in chairs everywhere we go all day every day leaves us crispy on one side and squishy on the other.

What's really fascinating is that anthropologists see similar

Nomads like the desert-dwelling Bedouin must live a minimalist lifestyle since excessive furniture is too cumbersome to travel with. Reclining, squatting, and sitting on the ground require a gentle baseline of activity that prevents them from completely disengaging. Remaining active in this way, the Bedouin are better protected from the harsh elements of their homeland.

postures and rest habits in pain-free people all over the world, meaning these postures are not owned by individual cultures. These postures were not created by the Bedouin. They are not yoga postures; they are *human* postures. They are the birthright of all human beings, an innate power to protect ourselves and amplify our abilities by maximizing the usefulness of our bodies through shape. As stated earlier, these instincts are demonstrated by developing children, even without any previous posture modeling to mimic. Just as we have instincts to begin rolling over, crawling, and eventually walking, we also have instincts as adults to cycle through positions that link these movement patterns together such as various sitting, kneeling, and squatting positions.

Just like a child, an indigenous person feels no shame in responding to the signals of their body even if it means sitting down in the dirt to rest or squatting to relieve themselves. Scientists are beginning to discover that these innate postures allow bodily functions to operate more efficiently, such as how squatting to defecate reduces effort and time to completion compared to sitting on a toilet. If we return to our roots by squatting to poop, we are performing a movement pattern that strengthens and mobilizes our body rather than creating one more slumpy seat to browse the internet from. If using a squatty potty is easier on our bodies than sitting on a toilet, what other functions operate more efficiently when we assume active rest postures?

I propose that all resting and digesting (or autonomic) functions of the human body can be optimized in some way through active rest and mindful breathing. Our instincts and ancient wisdom align in this matter, which can be witnessed by watching our children and our unadulterated contemporaries. Western societies may actually be in the minority with our postural practices, as Dr. Barone points out: "Evidence from eHRAF World Cultures also suggests that sitting and squatting appear to be far more common postures around the world than standing up straight or sitting with one's back vertically against a chair."

The human body was designed for movement. When we're not moving, our instincts drive us to rest in healthy shapes that allow us to conserve and create energy for future movements. But with a time crunch at work and no other options than to sit in a chair, we ignore our instincts for self-care. Let us consider for a moment how important instincts are to survival. Our hunter-gatherer ancestors would have been vulnerable to danger if they constantly reclined into passive rest shapes. If they disengaged their mental and physical alertness, they would have had less baseline awareness to act from when it was time to fight or flee. These basic human instincts to move throughout the day in response to the needs of the moment, to remain steadfast in mental alertness, and to rest in active postures are so strong that hunters of the Yaghan tribe have trouble standing still for long, even after miles of hiking through the rugged mountainous landscape of Tierra del Fuego:

> *They are somewhat unsteady when they stand; either their torsos are constantly swaying back and forth slightly, or they very inconspicuously move from one leg to the other.... They do not remain in an upright position for more than a few minutes. If they have a choice, they soon squat on the ground again, because they can rest better that way.*

If my main mode of transportation was vigorous hiking on constantly changing terrain, I would probably have trouble standing still for long too. Shifting weight into one leg to decompress the other would reduce my discomfort while keeping up a gentle activity so that I would not cool down entirely. If it became clear the group wasn't moving on anytime soon, I would take it as a cue to hunker down in an active rest posture. We must begin to tap into these basic human instincts and study the kinesthetic wisdom of pain-free-societies if

The Yaghan of Tierra del Fuego must hike long distances across rugged terrain to meet the needs of daily life. Given the opportunity, they prefer to rest in active shapes that counter the effects of their highly physical lifestyle.

we want to escape the shackles of chronic pain. So what's sitting in our way?

One obvious distinction between native peoples' settlements and modern living spaces is that the former has a noticeable lack of comfortable seating. Or perhaps it's more accurate to say that their homes lack modern furniture since these people find comfort with or without overstuffed armchairs. Without furniture, we have no choice but to use our body structure and environment for supporting work and rest. If we mold our homes and workplaces to be more like natural environments or native settlements, our instincts for self-care will be supported by our surroundings. Instead of furniture that is rigid, heavy, and immobile built with the intention of creating comfort through cushion, if we opt for more variable and portable types of furniture such as folding tables and chairs, we have the opportunity to change the shape of our environment throughout the day as it would if we were constantly on the move. Later on in this book you'll learn more about the use of variable furniture in order to make active resting postures more available in your life so you can work, rest, and play as nature intended.

Furniture won't be the only hurdle to climb over as you begin bringing active rest into your life. Just as it has become cool to slump, it has become quite strange to sit on the floor. I can't even perform a standing stretch at the gas station after hours of driving without people looking at me like I'm crazy. It can be assured that the first time you take your laptop down to the floor at work and lie on your belly as you read reports that your coworkers will either look at you like you're crazy or come over and ask you, "Is everything okay?" It has become the norm in our society to conform to certain shapes, and anyone taking shape outside the norm better be in the gym or a yoga class, or we will find it confusing and alarming. "Who's that person squatting at the bus stop? What's wrong with them? Why aren't they sitting on that perfectly good bench?" These questions are unique in the West, as other cultures consider these active postures not only normal but healthy as well.

Has this social pressure to conform our shape left our bodies deformed and incapable? When Western scientists immerse themselves in the practices of pain-free people, they find it hard to assimilate, noticing their bodies are inhibited from behaving in ways that make a wild landscape inviting, as ethnographer Waldemar Jochelson relates:

> *Even now, when the Aleut are familiar with the use of chairs and stools, many of them, particularly the women, perform their household tasks squatting on the floor. This is also the usual posture when at leisure.... The author was unable to attain such a position and always fell on his back when attempting to do so. To sit on the heels as do the Aleut one must have well developed leg-muscles capable of keeping the trunk in equilibrium.... Apparently the use of this posture by many generations of Aleut has made them adept at assuming it. Not only are they not fatigued thereby, but they seem to find it restful after their work.*

The gentle muscular activity derived from spending time in active rest postures such as the squat is a large part of what prevents common chronic pain among indigenous people. Jochelson's theory that healthy habits can be nurtured and passed on to future generations indicates that we too can offer our children a pain-free future by encouraging their instincts for active rest. It's important to note that this account was written in the 1920s when kinesthetic traditions in the West had just begun to deteriorate. Perhaps if the visit had occurred around the turn of the century, the Western visitor would have had more luck behaving like a local.

Beyond the physical differences between Jochelson and the pain-free people he studied, there was likely stark contrast between his tolerance for discomfort and theirs. Since modern living is cushioned by the comforts of technology and infrastructure, his daily exposure to discomfort was likely much lower than that of his native contemporaries. Ironically, it is this avoidance of discomfort that causes modern humans to endure much unnecessary suffering. Without the hardiness that comes from small doses of discomfort, we become overly sensitive. This makes us more likely to label discomfort in a new position as painful.

Case Study—Ruth

Ruth came to me because she felt overweight and weak and suffered from chronic hip pain. I offered that she try yoga therapy to help her discover the roots of her pain, but she chuckled and said, "Yoga isn't for me. Let's do personal training instead." I started Ruth on a gentle mobility and calisthenics program and monitored her movements to learn about her body. It was clear from watching her attempt a bodyweight squat that she had lost control of her hips. She would stumble back when trying to remain upright as she performed the movement. I decided it was safer to regress the exercise and encourage her to lean against a wall and slide down into a deep

The inability to assume basic human shapes like the squat limits physical health and can lead to more debilitating disabilities and chronic pain. Being able to get up off the ground through movements like the squat is an indicator of longevity.

squat position to stretch her hips, hoping this would help reconnect her mind to this part of her body. When I demonstrated the position, she looked at me in disbelief and said, "I'll never be able to do that."

With a little encouragement and a promise that I would keep her safe, Ruth leaned her back against the wall and started to slide down towards a squat. As she reached the edge of what her body was ready for, she looked up at me in surprise and said, "I had no idea my body was capable of this! It's hard to be here, but it feels kind of good at the same time," she said with a lighthearted grimace. "It's like the 'hurts so good' feeling of a massage."

I asked Ruth to remain at the edgy place and focus on taking five long slow breaths, paying close attention to how she was feeling. After a few moments, she came out with a groan and a sigh of relief.

2. *Returning to Our Roots*

"What did you notice while you stayed at the edge?" I asked after a few moments.

"It's funny, all I could think of was my time in the Philippines," she said while rubbing her head. "I could never find a place to sit down. There were no benches in the parks or at the bus stops. I was always so exhausted!" she exclaimed with a chuckle. "I saw people huddled in groups squatting on the ground and thought, 'These people are aliens....' But now I feel like I'm an alien living in someone else's body."

Ruth, like many Americans, had been shaped by the molds of our comfort-obsessed society. If she had been raised in the Philippines where chairs weren't necessary for finding rest, she may never have had to feel like an alien in her own body. She came to me seeking pain relief and weight loss through exercise but ended up having a therapeutic experience.

After finding some relief from our work together, Ruth brought her teenage son Michael in for a few sessions with me. Michael was athletic and full of energy, but he too had lost the ability to assume basic postures like the squat. Perhaps Michael had been shaped by the modeling he received from his mother. Maybe his track coach never showed him how to stretch after running dozens of miles a day. One thing is for sure: As a toddler he was a model for the perfect squat, as a picture Ruth showed me of young Michael playing in a sandbox demonstrated.

Michael lost capabilities he was born with. He too found his inability to squat without tipping backwards bewildering and admitted to his mother that his back was hurting while sitting through class at school. Ruth was mortified to learn that she was allowing her son to suffer and that she was perhaps contributing to his pain by passing down her unhealthy habits.

I didn't work with Ruth or Michael for very long. After completing a five-pack of personal training sessions, Ruth decided she wanted to walk the path on her own for a while. This is the case for many of my clients, most of whom will not return for future private sessions but might show up to group classes, or I might run into at the store. Some clearly gleaned useful knowledge from our work together and embody the benefits, while others report blankly, "I haven't done anything since our last session...." I wasn't sure if I got through to Ruth or not.

Three months later, I got an email from Ruth. Her daughter Melanie had just graduated from high school and was having a tough time coping with the transition. "I'd like to give Melanie some of your yoga therapy sessions, because she struggles with self-care and I'm really starting to worry about her," Ruth said in her email. "I'll come by on Monday and drop off a check to you at your new office."

I was working with another client when Ruth arrived, and I'm ashamed to say my jaw literally dropped when I saw her. She had lost so much weight and beamed with such confidence that I hardly recognized her! "Beth, what did you do to lose all this weight?" I asked.

"Well, basically all I did was cut out sugar like you recommended," she said, clearly pleased with herself. "And I still do my program three days a week."

"That's great to hear! How's your hip?"

"Well I'm not sure if it's the standing desk you convinced me to buy or the fact that I'm moving more, but my hips haven't bothered me in months," she said smiling. "The only time I notice discomfort that really grabs my attention is when I'm stretching. But I've grown to kind of like that feeling."

The more we experience and embrace healthy discomforts in our lives, the hardier we become. The hardier we become, the better we understand the difference between the type of discomfort that causes growth and that which leads to pain. This process teaches us the meaning of *therapeutic discomfort* by modifying our relationship with pain, helping us to understand its roots, and in turn how to end it.

3

Therapeutic Discomfort

"Once you start approaching your body with curiosity
rather than with fear, everything shifts."
—Bessel A. van der Kolk

The tendency to subsist at an unhealthy level of passivity and comfort in our modern lives stems from the cultural proclivity to check out of our inner experience. A plethora of screens and substances provide daily numbing that we mistake as rest. These distractions are quick and easy escapes from our problems and pain. Uncomfortable sensations feel so far away when we check out of ourselves and into something external. Of course we know deep down that this doesn't solve anything, but it's so much easier to check out than to check in.

Tough day at work? The television will help you forget. Big fight with a friend? You have thousands on your phone. Can't find a date? There's an app for that. Exhausted from housework? There's a robot for that. Excruciating pain? There's a new medical device for that. There's a narcotic for that. There's a surgery for that....

Technology promises us that it will free us from the bondage of the human form. That somehow a device, chemical, or procedure can solve our problems without us putting in any effort. But this is clearly not the case. In fact, quite the opposite is true. The more we rely on external sources of comfort, the more chronically uncomfortable we become. The most effective treatments for resolving physical pain and psychological stress require that the individual play an active role in their treatment.

As a yoga therapist, I meet a lot of people who are frustrated with their bodies and minds. They can't escape chronic pain or toxic thoughts and hope that yoga can help. I aid my clients in self-discovering shifts they instinctively know they need to make in order to transform. In yoga therapy we refer to these shifts as "action steps." Action steps are created by connecting what the client noticed in their yoga practice with the rest of their life. I've noticed that through their action steps, some clients' lives improve quickly and dramatically, while others seem to receive little to no long-term effects at all. The former eventually discontinue regular sessions as their self-practice has become strong enough to sustain itself. The latter often come back over and over seeking the acute benefits they receive from the sessions without ever achieving long-term change.

Many of my clients who don't achieve long-term benefits are very capable people who are deeply motivated to change. So I wondered for quite some time what was holding them back. A year after opening my yoga therapy practice, a distinct pattern began to emerge.

Case Study—Audrey

Audrey has been coming to me for weekly sessions for a couple of years. She is obese, carries a lot of tension, and suffers from what her doctors call "nerve pain." She has dabbled in all the services I offer: personal training, yoga therapy, and nutritional coaching. Her yoga therapy sessions are always powerful and moving. The action steps she creates sound so big that initially I was sure they would bring about healthy shifts. But week after week, she came back to me with the same pain to report and the same lack of lust for life. When asked how her action steps were going, sometimes she would report uninspiring success, and other times she would say something like, "Well, I just haven't gotten around to it yet." Or she would offer excuses explaining why she couldn't fit them into her life.

Even though she didn't appear to be accumulating any noticeable long-term benefits from our work together, Audrey kept coming back for sessions. She always seemed to leave feeling better than before. Then the COVID-19 pandemic hit. Our area was shut down in March. When I moved my sessions online, Audrey opted out. Her job was remote, and she didn't want any more screen time in her day.

3. Therapeutic Discomfort

That summer I did all of my yoga classes outdoors. One day Audrey showed up to my Yoga on the Beach class. I was amazed to see that she had lost a significant amount of weight. She told me that the pandemic had been good for her in a lot of ways because it forced her to focus on herself. Since she had discontinued working with me, as well as going to the doctor and the other alternative medicine practitioners she frequented, she noticed a shift.

"I realized I was asking everyone to heal me, but I wasn't willing to heal myself," she said with a laugh. "COVID gave me the time and permission to go inside, to hibernate on healing." Audrey went on to tell me all the ways the pandemic helped her to reinvent herself. She stopped eating out all the time, driving for hours for work, and of course going to yoga classes. "I had to do everything on my own. I had to do my practice without your help. At first it was so hard! Now it feels empowering."

Audrey recently reached out to me for online sessions. After the summer, she lost a bit of momentum. She was still controlling her weight well but was neglecting her movement practice. Her "nerve pain" was back. It was so intense she took a leave of absence from work.

Since returning to working with me, Audrey seems to have a different attitude on how the work can help her. Her action steps seem smaller, more digestible and doable. She asks for tangible tools to aid her self-practice, like short videos of our sessions to repeat on her own. She takes more time in-between our sessions and returns with more significant results to report.

From my experience working with Audrey I discovered an important piece of the self-healing puzzle. The main difference between people who accumulate long-term results when attempting to self-heal and those who only achieve acute benefits is that the former are not looking for someone else to fix them. They know that no one can create change for them other than themselves. No one can offer them a magic pill that will remove their pain. Pain-free people are willing to put in the work. Instead of relying on healing practitioners to solve their problems, they see them as conduits which help redirect their own efforts.

Just like a chiropractor or surgeon, a yoga therapist can be viewed as a magic pill that might be able to take pain away. But the power of yoga only encourages the body's natural ability to heal; it is not a remedy derived from some external source. Therefore, it is up to the individual to utilize the practice to activate natural healing processes within themselves often enough to effect real change. If you hope to transcend the pain and problems that plague you, you must become an active participant in your recovery plan. You must take an interest in yourself and find the curiosity to explore your body and mind rather than giving in to the urge to disconnect. You must be willing to encounter discomfort regularly and to mindfully modify the injured parts of yourself that reveal themselves through discomfort. No one can do this for you.

The Edge

The place where we are experiencing uncomfortable sensations or thoughts is called *the edge*, as in, "I'm at the edge of my comfort level. If I were to go any further too quickly or without paying careful attention, I could get hurt. I could go over the edge." Each edge we approach is an opportunity to enter into a captivating connection between body and mind. Through the discomfort we experience in the present, we can escape regrets of the past and anxieties of the future. This quality of the edge has immense therapeutic benefits, from healing physical pain to transcending psychological trauma. Each edge is like a fork in the path of healing where we can decide to lean in, back away, or ignore our experience. Unfortunately, most of us are choosing to ignore our edges more often. This is a major player in modern humans' tendency towards chronic pain and other lifestyle-based diseases.

Our bodies encounter physical and psychological edges constantly throughout the day, from the moment we fight to get ourselves out of bed in the morning to the moment we struggle to fall asleep at night. Every day we are faced with the edginess of being a sensitive and vulnerable creature on a planet that holds many dangers and wonders. Physical edges are the most obvious and easily recognized. They show up during physical activity as a burning in our muscles, increased heart rate, or achiness in an overtaxed joint. These edges are signals from our body to our mind to stay present in order to remain safe. Physical edges are present even at rest, such as when we have been lying on one side for too long. These more subtle edges encourage us to modify our position to avoid becoming "overcooked" on one side.

Psychological edges are less easily identified. However, they too manifest in our physical bodies when we think of or talk about something difficult. For example, when a discussion becomes heated, and we notice our face flushing and our muscles tensing. This is a physical indicator of our emotional edges. These edges are useful companions in our lives. When we're near mental and emotional edges, our body and mind are more closely connected, creating an opportunity for mindful shifts. We can use our perception of the edge to help us decide whether to lean in when things are feeling productive, or to de-escalate whatever is occurring and return to "working the edge" once we have collected ourselves. Working our psychological and emotional edges can help us to transcend the things that are holding us back. Whether you are trying to release pain from your physical body or to move past traumatic experiences, working these edges is a necessary part of your healing path.

Edges are present in our minds and bodies more frequently than we might notice. As we go through our day-to-day life, focusing on external distractions, we ignore the signals of our body and mind. This is especially true now that we have so many modes of checking-out available to us. On our daily commute, GPS replaces our natural sense of direction. Ads are hung strategically to block out the view of our environment and captivate our minds. On the subway we're so intimidated by legitimate social connections or so bored with ourselves that we plug our ears with headphones and watch videos until we reach our destination. Technology gives us an immediate check-out from our bodies, our minds, our neighbors, and any chance of interacting with life as humans were intended to. We must become more mindful of how we interact with technology if we want to live less dysfunctional lives.

If you suffer from chronic pain, one way you may have learned to deal with your discomfort is to "put it out of your mind." Maybe as you focus on work or otherwise move mindlessly through your day, the pain signals decrease, so you can forget about them until you are at rest again and the signals inevitably increase their volume. If you

"Tech neck" is a nasty learned posture that we develop while texting and typing for long periods of time. Shapes like this demonstrate a total disconnect from our body and cause us a great deal of pain.

consistently suppress or dismiss pain signals, nothing can be done to heal them. Soon they will grow into something much worse.

Post-traumatic stress disorder (PTSD) is an extreme but useful example to consider. In a traumatized person's body, the traumatic events are still occurring in the present moment. All the anguish they felt, and all the fear and anxiety that they have endured after the fact, combine to create a truly tortuous and seemingly inescapable experience. People with PTSD experience physical and mental edges daily because their body and mind are constantly reliving the events that traumatized them. The cycle of reliving the events is the body and mind's attempt to figure out what happened so they can move on. Without facing these edges with a therapeutic lens in hand to help them process and heal, their discomforts continue chronically. Their body and mind cannot let go of the pain trapped within the past. However, if the individual is willing to physically and mentally encounter their trauma again in a controlled environment under the guidance of a professional, they can learn that they are safe in the present moment. They can teach their body and mind that they are no longer living in their traumatic past. Repeated regularly, this approach has been shown to be the most effective long-term care plan for treating PTSD.

Whether or not you have PTSD, you have certainly experienced trauma in some way over the course of your life, be it physical, mental, or both. The signals your subconscious sends to your body and mind may be gentler than those of someone living in the throes of PTSD, but these edges still have a significant effect on your daily life. Gentle edges that go unaddressed too long are like a dead mouse that the cat dragged behind the couch. Eventually it begins to stink. Left alone long enough, it can become poisonous.

This hidden poison stored within us is why we have emotional reactions in response to physical release. It's why many people report feeling inexplicably weepy after a good massage or on top of the world after a good run. It's why dancing, singing, and other forms of self-expression feel so cathartic. It's why a smell from our past can bring on a sense of ourselves that we thought was lost long ago, and how an old song can cause a symphony of emotions and familiar yet forgotten sensations from when we first heard that tune.

The massage, the run, the smell, the song,

Moving our bodies can cause a cascade of sensations and emotions that vary from uncomfortable to euphoric. In this way the physical body acts as a gateway to our subtle layers, providing the opportunity to process current life circumstances and past traumas.

these are all just vectors of redirection that return us to focusing on ourselves. This allows us to release the story of our past so that we can focus on the present moment. Focusing on the present we realize we are free from our past afflictions and need not worry about the future. With these insights, we find peace—peace that facilitates the natural healing capabilities of our bodies.

Case Study—Kate

Kate was a chronic low back pain sufferer and single mom of two. She always put others first and didn't accept help easily. When she first left the father of her children, she found that she could escape the pain he had caused her by burying herself in her job and homemaking. She protected her injured heart under folded arms, furrowed brow, and hunched shoulders. She ignored her inner experience in order to maintain her focus on being a strong provider and caregiver.

As a chef, Kate was on her feet all day and constantly bending over to pick things up. With her protective posture in place, she could not walk, stand, or lift things in healthy alignment. One day at work, Kate's back pain became unbearable. She tried to push through the pain, but her boss noticed she was becoming distracted and clumsy. He saw her as a liability and sent her home. This happened on and off over the course of a year, and eventually, Kate got fired.

This was when I met Kate. She had gotten a reduced fee membership at the YMCA I was working at and came into one of my yoga classes seeking relief. At the time I was offering free yoga therapy sessions as a part of my training. Kate approached me after class and said that she enjoyed the practice and signed up for a yoga therapy session. In our first session, Kate told me that she was forced to apply for unemployment and was dealing with a lot of financial stress. She was afraid to go to the doctor because she didn't have health insurance. She stayed at home most of the day until her kids got out of school, hoping that rest would ease her pain. I noticed how hard it was for Kate to relax her shoulders away from her ears, an instinctive way of protecting the neck. She spent most of the session protecting her chest by either folding her arms or hugging one arm with the other. Shapes that could be useful in fending off a physical attack had become her natural state of being. Her body had become a shield to protect her heart. Her emotions, unable to dissipate, hid out in her body as physical tension and caused her intense pain.

I asked Kate how comfortable she was with physical touch. "The only people who touch me are my kids," she said with a chuckle. "I'm nervous, but I think I could really use some bodywork." With this sentiment in mind, I felt compelled to alert Kate to the difference between a yoga therapy session and a massage. I explained that there may be emotional connections to the physical pain she was experiencing and that emotions may be stirred up by touching upon the parts of her that were hurt.

"You might experience thoughts, feelings, or emotions connected to the physical sensations during your session," I said. "Or you may find that your stretching or my touch triggers memories. These are important things to notice. When you do, speak to them. I'll prompt you to speak often in your session." Kate nodded with understanding.

To begin her session I directed Kate through deep breathing and posture modification. I encouraged her to change her shape from closed to open and to notice how it changed her breath. After just a few moments of being bigger, Kate began to weep softly. I asked her what she was noticing.

"I haven't let anyone look this closely at me in a long time," she choked out under suppressed sobs. "I feel worthless. Like why would anyone ever

When we are anxious, fearful, or depressed, we embody our feelings through protective postures. Just like other learned postures, these shapes can become ingrained in habit. Over time they deform our bodies and trap us in a cycle of physical and emotional pain that exacerbate one another.

give a shit about me?" As the emotion began to take over her body, her protective shape began to return. I encouraged Kate to stay with her feelings, to combine them with the larger shape, and to breathe deeply. "I'll try!" she exclaimed with a look of pained effort on her face.

For a few minutes, this made Kate sob uncontrollably. In the throes of her experience, she would revert to her protective shape and then fight to broaden her body again. She would sob as she reverted back to a slump and then sit up and take big breaths as she attempted to regain her composure. I felt like I was witnessing an argument between two roommates living in one body. One was saying, "We need to hide!" and the other was saying, "I'm tired of hiding!"

After a few minutes, Kate calmed herself. She blew her nose and wiped her tears away with a tissue, then returned to a tall posture. Her breath was a bit inhibited by her clogged nose, so I encouraged her to breathe through her mouth if necessary. "Okay, I'm ready to continue," she said with conviction. I proceeded to guide Kate through some warming movements that targeted her shoulders, neck, and back. Despite her initial sorrow, she seemed quite pleased to be moving her body. I then led her through some basic stretches for the areas she mentioned wanting to address. When I asked her what she was noticing in these shapes, she offered benign feedback like, "I feel a good stretch here."

We then entered into the assisted stretching portion of the practice. Since we had just met and I was still in training, I decided less would be more. I was cautious of triggering her domestic abuse trauma through my touch, as she had already had a big enough experience at the start of her session. Instead of taking her into a deep stretch, I returned her to the seated shape she started in. I stood behind her with my lower leg against her spine, placed my hands on her shoulders, and helped her roll her shoulders back. There was a lot of tension fighting the shape, but through her breathing she gradually began to open up. "What's different about this pose now?" I asked.

"A part of me wants to cry again," Kate murmured with a crackling voice. "But I also feel like I don't have any tears left. I feel like I can breathe again, and it feels *so* good. I don't need to cry!" she said with a chortle. "And it feels really good to be supported here."

While she stayed in the position, I asked Kate what her support system was like. She said that since the divorce friends and family had been reaching out to her, but she hadn't been letting them in.

"I think this closed body I've created doesn't allow others in," she said. "I want to accept the help, but I don't know how. Even though he could be really mean, my ex also supported me in many ways. Since the divorce, I haven't been able to let anyone in. I feel like I have to do it all on my own."

I reflected back to Kate my interpretation of what she said. She nodded in agreement. I then guided her to lie down. I gave Kate some passive stretch assists similar to those offered in Thai massage. I pulled on her legs, arms, and neck for traction and gave her a gentle head rub. Then I let her rest for a few minutes with no touch. After her relaxation, I guided Kate to return to a seated position. Without any reminders, she sat tall and took some deep breaths. I asked her to reflect back on her practice and share with me what she gleaned.

Kate told me her interpretation of her experience. She felt that she was protecting herself from others so that she couldn't get hurt again. "But in doing so, I've been hurting myself," she said. "I don't want to be closed off all the time. I don't want to be one of those guarded people. And I definitely don't want to be in pain all the time." Kate went on to create an action step of sitting in meditation for a few minutes every morning. She said she also wanted to reach out to her parents and let them know what she was going through. Kate asked me to recommend stretches she could do for her shoulders, as it was her intuition that her body pain originated there. I offered her instead a simple biofeedback practice.

"Anytime you notice your pain returning, or if you're feeling closed off from others, check in with your shoulders," I offered. "Notice if they're hunched up, and if so, simply roll them back and down. Take a deep breath every time you do. Notice what happens next."

I didn't see Kate again for a couple of weeks. When she came into another yoga class, I noticed something was different about her. Her skin tone had darkened, her resting posture had shifted, and her eyes had more life in them. Before the class, she was talking with some other women, and she seemed to be having a nice conversation, so I waited until after class to check in with her.

Part One—Discovering the Roots of Our Pain

It was wonderful to see Kate's movement practice. She moved with the same conviction I witnessed in her session after her initial emotional release. During the resting posture at the end of class, she looked very content. After class Kate told me that since our session, she had mustered up the courage to accept some help from her family. Her dad gave her a loan to fix her car, and a friend helped her get a new cooking position at the restaurant they worked at. Kate said she only meditated a few times, but she did the biofeedback exercise every day.

"Ari, you saved my life!" she exclaimed. I shook my head no.

"Kate, you walked into the Y because you knew you needed a change," I reminded her. "You first lived out the yet uncreated action step of reaching out for help when you applied for a discounted membership and scheduled a free session. You did all the work. I was just your witness."

If we listen closely to the signals of our body and mind as we encounter edges, we will notice an intuition that our efforts within discomfort will benefit us in some way. This is known as *therapeutic discomfort,* the uncomfortable sensation of healthy stressors. We can become friends with this type of discomfort. Doing so will build strength of character, physical stamina, hardiness, and heightened mental fortitude.

The practice of active rest is just one of the many tools at our disposal for transcending our pain and transforming our trauma through therapeutic discomfort. Each body experiences therapeutic discomfort differently. Different postures will produce more or less sensation depending on who you are, what you have been through, and how you've dealt with it. When practicing active rest, some people will rediscover old injuries, uncover limitations, or find that certain shapes feel completely unavailable to their body. Others will discover they were blessed with natural flexibility or other genetic advantages, but this does not mean that one person's journey is less significant than another's.

Your journey may seem much more challenging than others. Your disease, handicap, or traumatic life experiences may make you feel like you were dealt a bad hand. This might cause you frustration on your healing journey and even encourage you to give up. When encountering this kind of frustration, consider the inspiring feats of individuals like Christopher Reeve and Stephen Hawking. Know that the stronger the shackles of your body or mind, the more strength you will build as you overcome adversity; that the greater the limitations of your current situation, the more relief you will feel as you overcome the rigors set before you; that the more of an underdog you appear to be, the more people you will inspire with the fact that you were able to transcend your troubles.

In order to begin your journey of transformation, you will need to sharpen a set of tools given to you at birth, tools that you may have neglected since childhood because you stopped listening to your self-preservation instincts. Maybe you lost touch with these instincts because no one encouraged the preservation of them, or life got in the way of taking care of yourself. Or perhaps you've simply forgotten how.

Mindful Breathing

All of this talk about "active rest" and "therapeutic discomfort" sounds like a lot of work, and you're a busy person with lots on your plate. How can you be expected to find the time and energy to deal with the pain lurking inside your body and mind? That's why we check out in the first place. It's so much easier, and it feels like we are preserving our energy. But the more we check out, the more our energy reserves are sapped, and the cycle of pain and checking out perpetuates itself. Luckily, humans are armed with a hidden superpower that gives us the ability to defeat our pain and recreate energy. But we have to be willing to take the time and make the effort to utilize it.

Mindful breathing is the practice of focusing on your breath to create a mind-body connection. Focused breathing slows mental chatter and allows us to remain present to our edges. When fully present, it is much easier to find the inner truth available at the edge, which leads to transformation. Mindful breathing has been proven effective at alleviating many treatment-resistant conditions such as chronic stress, depression, anxiety, mental illness, insomnia, and addiction. It can aid in digestion, promote focus and comprehension, calm restless children, improve heart and lung health, enhance brain function, fortify the immune system, and activate superhuman strength and stamina.

The list of benefits derived from consistently practicing mindful breathing goes on and on. But what is most relevant within this context is whether or not mindful breathing can help us to combat chronic pain. Research on this front is very promising. Let's examine three studies that when compared to one another offer insight on the cumulative benefits of mindful breathing.

In a study outlined in *PAIN*, researchers examined whether breath rate affected pain symptoms and associated emotions in women suffering from fibromyalgia. By simply slowing their breathing to half the normal rate, participants noted a marked decrease in their pain levels when stimulated by a heat applicator. They also reported a more even mood state than they normally associate with pain.[1] It's interesting to note that the participants had little to no experience with mindfulness practices before this study. This indicates that mindful breathing is a useful pain management tool even to practitioners who are just embarking on their mindfulness journey.

Another study from *Nursing and Midwifery* sought to discover whether mindfulness practices could affect pain from tension-based migraine headaches. The study's organizers empowered participants with simple mindful breathing practices in an eight-week course. At the end of the eight weeks,

Mindful breathing is a meditative practice that has been shown to alleviate pain, improve mood, and increase our sense of self control. Breathing mindfully is an essential part of the practice of active rest and of living a life free from pain.

the participants reported significantly reduced stress, improved mental health, dramatically reduced pain, and a decrease in the incidence of headaches.[2] When compared to the acute benefits of mindful breathing demonstrated by the aforementioned study, this evidence indicates that long-lasting benefits can be accumulated through consistent practice.

A study published in *Psychosomatic Medicine* aimed to determine whether meditation practitioners have greater pain tolerance than non-meditators. Meditators with at least 1,000 hours of experience and a control group of volunteers were asked to report their perceptions of pain when stimulated with a heat applicator, much like the women in the first study. It was found that the meditators required significantly higher temperatures of heat application in order to label the sensation they were experiencing as pain compared to the control group. Through concentration the meditators were able to decrease their perceived pain once it occurred, whereas concentrating increased perception of pain in non-meditators. The researchers also noted, "In meditators, pain modulation correlated with slowing of the respiratory rate and with greater meditation experience."[3] Additionally, the meditators reported a higher tendency to be observant of and nonreactive to the heat, indicating that they were able to perceive the pain without being as sensitive to it as non-meditators.

I present to you a summary of these three articles in hopes of conveying two important ideas: (1) that mindful breathing has the power to immediately alleviate your pain and (2) that practicing mindful breathing regularly over the course of your lifetime will gradually improve your hardiness and decrease your sensitivity to pain. Combined with the other benefits of mindful breathing mentioned before and the fact that it is always available to us at no cost, this practice has the power to change lives. As you embark upon your journey of self-healing, mindful breathing will be your greatest tool for controlling the level of therapeutic discomfort you will discover in active rest.

The most basic and perhaps most useful mindful breathing practice is to simply shift all of your awareness towards your breath. Especially at first, practice mindful breathing someplace where there are few distractions. Lie down on the ground if you can, or sit on the floor with your back against a wall for support. With consistent practice in a controlled environment, the benefits will become available to you anywhere, at any time, in any shape.

While practicing this kind of mindful breathing, there's no need to try to change how deep you are breathing. Instead, simply take note of sensations connected to your breathing. Be equally observant of both the pleasant and unpleasant sensations you experience while attempting to be still. Frequently your mind will drift away from the breath and back to internal dialogue. This does not mean you are failing to breathe mindfully. It just means you are human, and you are training yourself to put down one tool before picking up another. Thoughts are not necessarily the enemy of meditation. Some of our most profound insights are available to us within the meditative state. When thoughts that aren't useful break your focus, don't reprimand yourself. Instead, simply recognize the drift in your focus, and return it to your breath. This is the essence of meditation.

The practice mentioned above is just one of the hundreds of mindful breathing exercises that have been utilized for millennia by our ancestors for a multitude of reasons—reasons ranging from pure boredom to seeking pain relief to bringing more awareness to the present moment. The mind-body connection created by mindful breathing is useful to different people in different ways. Different breath practices can be utilized to create different effects. Some produce more alert heat-based energy, while others help to calm and cool.

Practice—Three-Part Breath

I have outlined below the breathing practice I think is most useful for facilitating the active rest method. Three-part breath is designed to activate all of the parts of your body that aid the action of breathing. Exaggerating your breath in this way will help you to direct sensations where you want them while in active rest postures. It will also ensure you have plenty of energy for working the edge. Most importantly, this deeper breathing pattern will teach your nervous system that you are safe within the postures and safe within the present moment. Practice three-part breath every day if you can, even if it's just for a few minutes. This will create a foundational perspective on the effectiveness of mindful breathing for modifying your inner experience. Practice first with eyes open as you read; then repeat it with eyes closed, and see if you notice a difference:

1. Notice your resting breath pattern without seeking to intentionally change it. As you send your awareness towards your breath, notice if it changes on its own simply by being watched.

2. Exaggerate the natural shifts that occurred as you began noticing your breath. If your breath naturally deepened or lengthened when you first began to watch it, encourage these qualities to increase incrementally with each breath cycle.

3. Imagine your breath filling and emptying three chambers: belly, ribs, and chest. Inhaling first to your belly, then your ribs, then your chest. Exhaling from the ribs first, then the chest, then the belly. Use your mind to follow the breath through your body and to inspect the sensations coming up.

4. Once you are comfortable with the three-part breath practice, use it to help reshape your posture. You can do this in many postures. Try it first seated, with no back support if possible. On your inhales, imagine a string attached to the crown of your head pulling you straight up. On your exhales, relax your shoulders away from your ears. Add in the biofeedback exercises you've already learned: as you inhale, tip the bucket of your pelvis forward; as you exhale, gently squeeze your shoulder blades together. Repeat this process as long as you like. Each inhale grow taller; each exhale relax where you can while maintaining the shape. Notice how breathing in this way affects your posture and how the big posture facilitates further deepening of the breath.

5. Finally, try to even out the length of the inhales and exhales, keeping them slow and controlled. You can do this by counting four or five beats as you inhale, and counting the same as you exhale. Make sure that you are inhaling fully and exhaling completely, without straining or forcing the breath.

For a guided three-part breath practice and to learn more ways to combine mindful breathing with the practice of active rest visit the *Burn Your Chair* bonus resource guide at *www.burnyourchair. com.*

Mindful breathing is a practice of active rest in and of itself, as it restores more energy than it burns. If you breathe mindfully while in active rest postures, you can direct your breath towards targeted tissues for additional benefits. ***Directional breathing*** is the practice of guiding the ebb and flow of air pressure created by your breath to specific parts of the body. For instance, if you are in a squat position, you can massage the muscles of the low back and hips by focusing your breath in the belly. In the hanging position, focusing inhales into the chest and upper back will encourage these areas to relax more fully when exhaling. This practice requires a familiarity with three-part breath, which trains your ability to send the breath where you want it. You'll learn more about how to combine the practice of mindful breathing with active rest postures in Part Two.

Just as we have instincts from an early age to experiment with active rest postures, we also have an instinct to play with our breath, specifically, using our breath to modify the functions of our nervous system. In response to stress, our nervous system sends out signals to quicken heart rate, breath rate, and mobilize other systems to prepare us to fight or flee. Instinctively, we may attempt to relieve some of our stress and slow these effects by taking in a deep breath or letting out a sigh. Instincts like these can be harnessed and amplified through the practice of mindful breathing.

When I was ten, my father bought me a video game called Resident Evil. It was a very violent game set in a post-apocalyptic world, and your mission was to eradicate a zombie plague. Much like a horror movie, the bad guys pop out when you least expect it. I remember literally jumping out of my seat in terror many times. It really put me on edge, which of course was the intention of the game. I couldn't calm down after I stopped playing. My nervous system was staying prepared for battle. At night, every creaky floorboard and distant cat meow put me on high alert. I couldn't get to sleep. Sometimes the fear would well up so much that I would take a big gasping breath and hold it in, periodically sipping in air until I felt like I was going to pop.

When my mother found out about the game, she threw it away. But the fear followed me for some time. Each night for the next few months, when I would get scared, I played with my breath. I would hold my breath in, hold my breath out, take big breaths, take rapid short-sharp breaths, and experiment with making my breath as long as possible. All of these experimental practices almost perfectly model traditional yogic breath techniques that have been used for encouraging optimal well-being for thousands of years. Eventually my instinctive breath practice became a nightly bedtime visualization. The experiences varied in exact detail, but most often I rode a magic carpet over a desert city. My imagination was so powerful that I could feel my stomach drop as the carpet took dips and dives. This was also the only time in my life when I was capable of lucid dreaming.

Even though I ventured down a path of checking out of myself and into screens, my childhood instincts and imagination were still strong enough to aid me in transcending minor traumas. At the time, I wasn't worried that I wouldn't be able to get to sleep. Instead, I deeply gave into and enjoyed immensely the feeling of being exhausted and noticed the restfulness of just lying there. It was so relieving that I would fight to keep myself awake as long as I could to continue enjoying relaxing. As I continued into puberty, these tools were replaced by a yearning to fit in, which meant pushing my parents for more violent video games and more channels on the TV. Eventually, my breath practice was completely erased. I couldn't imagine myself flying, and I no longer enjoyed just lying in bed. My instinctive self-care tools began to disappear. Anxiety, depression, fear, and pain began to replace them. It wasn't until recently that I replaced practices of checking out with the practice of checking in and began to see again the power always inside me.

It's too bad so many of us lose ourselves in this way, disconnecting habitually for so long that it eventually causes our bodies and minds to fall apart. Yet there does seem to be benefits to this painful process. The journey of transformation from whole to broken to whole again may leave scars, but it can also create strength, wisdom, and deepen our sense of empathy.

When starting a breath practice, you will need to tap into the instinct to play with and be curious about sensations. You most likely lost touch with this instinct during early adulthood. Don't hold too tightly to the idea that there are "right" and "wrong" ways of practicing mindful breathing. Through free-flowing experimentation, you will discover that different ways of breathing will alter your perception of discomfort. Over time, you will discover the types of mindful breathing that best facilitate your own well-being.

Mindful breathing will be your anchor for remaining present while in active rest postures. It will be your control over the "volume" of your experience. The seesaw action of your inhales and exhales manipulates the body's tissues through changes in air pressure within your body. When you inhale, you increase the air pressure in your body, which adds length to your tissues and stimulates your energy systems. As you exhale, you release the air pressure, creating spaciousness and activating the part of your nervous system that encourages relaxation. The practice of exaggerating the qualities of your breath will increase these effects. If you choose to move into the spaces that open up within you through your mindful breathing, your body and mind will grow, and your attachments to the past and fears of the future will begin to disappear.

4

There Is Nothing Wrong with You

"Sometimes folk medicine is more sensible than modern medicine."
—John Sarno M.D., *Mind Over Back Pain*

The failing of modern medicine is that we treat sick people like malfunctioning machines. If there is pain present in the body, there must be something wrong with the body. Healing then is about "fixing" the body's parts through surgery or ameliorating the body's faulty chemical processes through medicine. Why then are so many patients stuck in a revolving door of chronic symptoms and doctor's visits?

Human beings are more complex than any machine ever created. Therefore this idea that pain and disease are only symptoms of physical dysfunction is as old and tired as our medical system itself. Western doctors are primarily trained in allopathy. This means they treat symptoms with remedies rather than seek to prevent them. Symptoms are generally treated singularly without much regard to how or why they developed. Patients are seen as problems to fix with haste in order to ensure a steady stream of customers return again and again in their pursuit of relief.

The problem cannot be blamed entirely on the medical system. It is a cultural phenomenon that physical pain is acceptable, normal, easy to talk about and fix, whereas psychological, emotional, and spiritual pain are taboo topics too uncomfortable to talk about. This cultural inclination to focus on the physical and neglect the emotional and spiritual modifies the medical market, influencing which treatments and interventions are made available and affordable. It also affects the decisions made by health insurance companies regarding

Western medicine is a system of "sick care," not health care. Rather than attempting to prevent illness through education and lifestyle, doctors are assigned the task of fixing broken bodies. This trains us to think that pain indicates there is something wrong with us. Instead of changing how we live, we wait until the pain returns and ask our doctor for the next surgery or medication that will take the pain away.

which treatments they will cover. Doctors are seen as "progressive" and "crunchy" if they suggest that symptoms are stress or trauma related. And they stand to lose a patient's faith completely if they suggest psychological or emotional pain could be at the root of a physical problem.

There are many common pathologies that are known to be caused or at least influenced by stress and tension. Ulcers, hay fever, asthma, heart disease, obesity, diabetes, headaches, depression, anxiety, GERD, IBS, Alzheimer's disease, accelerated aging and premature death can all be linked to emotional and psychological well-being. Many "progressive" doctors and scientists now suggest that the mind has more influence over the body than previously thought and that a whole host of psychosomatic symptoms are cause for many trips to the doctor. Yet the treatments offered only address the physical dysfunction, not the underlying mental or emotional issues. Unfortunately, most doctors are not well equipped or educated enough to successfully diagnose and treat patients with such symptoms. This leaves many people trapped in the medical system for years, never receiving the type of care that will help them achieve long-lasting results.

The idea, "there must be something wrong with my body if my body is in pain," is one of the main things causing the problem in the first place, according to pain specialist Dr. John Sarno. In his book, *Mind Over Back Pain*, Sarno says that much of our pain is created by emotional tension which manifests itself physically.[1] Medical diagnoses are often made from X-rays and MRIs that show some structural abnormality, and the physician equates the pain or dysfunction with the presence of the abnormality. Sarno suggests that diagnoses and prognoses like these generate fear and anxiety in patients which worsens their stress and tension, leading to more pain. If instead, the patient was guided to accept that the abnormality is part of who they are and simply worked to reduce their stress and tension, they would have a quicker and more complete resolution to the problem.

Let's consider Kate again, still in the throes of her chronic back pain. She goes to the doctor seeking relief instead of seeking guidance on beginning a self-healing journey. Her doctor orders an X-ray. The X-ray comes back to show slight scoliosis of her spine and the beginnings of disc degeneration. Her doctor tells her that she will need surgery and suggests that she stop all physically demanding activities until well after her recovery. Shocked by the severity of her diagnosis and the implications to her life as a single mom, Kate panics. With increased anxiety and no physical activity to burn off her tension comes an exacerbation of her pain, and she is convinced surgery is her only option.

Now let's imagine another scenario. What if instead of a preemptive X-ray, Kate's doctor had a face-to-face visit with her? If he had a close enough relationship with her as we hope a primary care physician would, he surely would have noticed that she didn't seem herself and that she looked uncharacteristically stressed. "Have you experienced any major life changes recently?" he might ask.

"Well, I divorced my husband a few months back," Kate says sheepishly.

"Was it an amicable separation?" the doctor asks.

"No, not really...." Kate says, hanging her head and rubbing her shoulder. "What does this have to do with my back?"

"Kate, sometimes body pain is triggered by emotional pain or stress," her doctor says, typing some notes. "I'd like to prescribe you a round of physical therapy and refer you to a psychotherapist before we do any unnecessary scans."

"So, you don't think there's anything wrong with me?"

"Kate, you're only human."

In the second scenario in which the doctor prescribes a holistic pain treatment plan, there was no assumption that there was something physically wrong with Kate. He hypothesized instead that her sudden onset of chronic pain was triggered by tension built up from traumatic life circumstances. Without receiving a terrifying medical diagnosis of some structural abnormality causing her pain, Kate was offered the opportunity to self-heal through therapeutics. This avoided her fearing for weeks another major trauma like surgery and spending months or years recovering. There was no seed of "there's something wrong with you" planted in her mind that grew into fear, distress, and an exacerbation of physical tension.

Dr. Sarno suggests that people like Kate have physical pain that is generated by emotional tension, a condition he calls Tension Myositis Syndrome, or TMS. He suggests that some people are more susceptible to the symptoms of TMS because of their tendency to hold on to tension. Sarno argues this tension chokes off the blood and oxygen supply to affected muscle and nerve cells, causing tenderness and pain. Patients with previous diagnoses, history of surgery, and long-term use of pain medication have resolved their pain through Dr. Sarno's mind-body approach. This suggests that the pain relief some find from surgery is merely a placebo effect: "the ultimate placebo," says Sarno. The patient's belief that they have been fixed relieves some tension and offers them temporary relief until stress and tension inevitably pile up again. Then, more surgery and medicine are prescribed, and the cycle continues. Sarno goes as far as to suggest that most common spinal pathologies are not the cause of pain for many people who receive these diagnoses, that conditions such as degeneration of the spinal discs are completely normal and that the body is capable of adapting to these conditions without chronic pain.

Dr. Sarno has written four books on his mind-body approach to healing chronic pain, as well as contributed to many journal publications. Study data from hundreds of patients referred to him show that an overwhelming majority (around 90 percent) of patients found relief through his treatment plan. Subsequent independent studies have continued to demonstrate the value of his method, which consists mainly of education around the nature of TMS. Patients who are able to accept their TMS diagnosis get better quickly, whereas those who resist the diagnosis maintain persistent symptoms of chronic pain.

To find relief from TMS, sufferers need only to accept that there is nothing wrong with them and to address the underlying mental/emotional issues triggering their body pain. There are three therapeutic modalities that have proven to be most useful in aiding recovery from TMS: physical therapy, psychotherapy, and mindfulness practice. Physical therapy has been shown to be successful because it strengthens our sense of self-control and self-efficacy. It creates an understanding that we have control over our pain. Psychotherapy is useful for addressing the underlying mental and emotional issues that cause TMS. It allows the patient to vent their tension and to stop it from resurfacing by understanding its roots. Mindfulness practices shine a light on the connection between body and mind, offering a combination of the effects of physical therapy and psychotherapy.

Dr. Sarno agrees that these modalities are useful, but his method does not offer them initially. Instead, it simply educates patients on the theory of TMS and the idea that accepting a TMS diagnosis leads to self-healing. If Dr. Sarno is correct, in essence, we are creating much of our own suffering. This idea may sound depressing, but it can actually be liberating. It means we hold the power to cure our own pain. If we are creating much of our own suffering through our suppressed emotions, then we can escape our suffering by encouraging the health of our mental and emotional bodies.

Body Language

The mind and body are in constant communication. Most of this communication occurs on a subconscious level. Oftentimes our conscious mind is not a part of the conversation; instead, it is focused on thoughts of the past or future. Since we spend most of our time thinking and not focusing on the present moment, we don't notice the conversation constantly happening between our body and mind. Why then is it so easy for others to pick up on subtle hints that we are in need of attention? How can other people notice our discomfort even before we notice it ourselves?

The answer is simple: our bodies do not lie. If there is something wrong on the inside, it will be displayed on the outside. Dr. Sarno's approach to healing chronic pain is successful because he encourages sufferers to become active participants in their journey to recovery. He asks that they unite their body and mind rather than see them as separate. In yoga therapy we believe that the shape and behavior of our bodies are reflections of the shape and behavior of our minds,

that if we are feeling guarded, this can be easily seen through the way we arrange our face and posture. It's not a hard concept to grasp; folded arms, hunched back, and downward curling eyebrows are all obvious signs that something is wrong. Open chest, tall spine, and upward curving lips are signs of a positive mood state.

Conventional wisdom has touted for centuries the power of the smile to improve our mood and lift our spirits even when we're feeling down or times are hard. There's a powerful human instinct to encourage others to smile or laugh when

Reshaping our embodiment is as simple as smiling. Research indicates that our facial expression has a strong effect on our mood. When our mood improves, our posture follows; therefore, smiling is an important practice on the path to healing chronic pain.

they're feeling sad. Science is beginning to support this ancient practice. A recent meta-analysis of more than 138 studies and 11,000 participants from all over the world demonstrated that facial expressions have a measurable influence over our mood.[2] Smiling can make us feel better, and scowling can make us feel worse through changes in the nervous and endocrine systems. Yet the phrase "turn that frown upside down" is likely to be met with rage more than newfound cheerfulness. Therefore smiling is something that must be practiced and reinforced often, not forced out of us in moments of despair.

Practice—Smiling

Try this simple smiling practice. Like other practices in the book, it requires focused self-awareness. For this reason, it will be helpful to read the practice first, and then try it on with eyes closed. To be guided in this practice, watch the "embodiment exercises" video included in the bonus resource guide at www.burnyourchair.com.

1. Sit on the floor with your back against a wall, or lie down on the ground. Check in with your resting body, noticing any effort or ease in this posture. Notice thoughts, feelings, and emotions without placing any judgment.
2. Gradually shift all of your awareness to your breath.
3. While paying attention to your breath, smile! Notice what happens within you when you smile. What happens to your breath? What sensations do you experience?
4. Next, shake off the smile, and return to a restful facial expression. Notice breathing again, and frown. How does frowning land in your body?
5. Finally, try this breathing exercise. As you inhale, frown, and as you exhale, smile. How does that feel? Next try it in the opposite way. Smile as you inhale, and frown as you exhale. Does one pattern feel more natural than another? What does this teach you about your body and your breath?

If subtle changes in the shape of our face can cause subtle changes in our mood or in our breath, could postural changes produce similar effects on a greater scale? If it were possible to smile with our whole body, would this help us to manage our emotions in order to break the physical tension that binds us with chronic pain?

When we are anxious or stressed, our body becomes tense. Tension costs a lot of energy, leaving us with little left over for protecting ourselves. If we're not being mindful, this will cause us to crumple into a slump. This kind of disengaged posture compresses our abdomen, thereby inhibiting our breath. Our brain perceives any suppression of our breath as a signal that we are unsafe and generates feelings of anxiety to communicate to the conscious mind that something is wrong. If we do not maintain a strong mind-body relationship through regular mindfulness practice, we generally ignore these edges. This creates a negative feedback loop in which the brain continues generating anxiety alarm bells that go unanswered, leading to more tension and more posture-produced pain.

This experience can be easily witnessed by those around us. The kind of shapes we take when we're suffering from negative emotions communicate that we are weak, closed off, and unwell. If instead we arrange ourselves in a way that encourages the fullness of our breath, our shape naturally communicates to others that we are safe and in control. Even if we are experiencing negative emotions, this practice has the power to signal the brain that we are safe, which will downregulate the body's stress response. Within shapes that the brain perceives as safe, feelings of easefulness and alertness arise. Through this easeful and alert state, we are more capable of addressing our inner experience so that we can escape the cycle of emotional tension that generates physical pain. This creates a positive feedback loop in which mindful breathing gives way to easeful sorting of emotional baggage, allowing us the opportunity to prevent tension at the source. Again, this inner experience is easily witnessed on the outside, as the shapes we make when we are in control send a message to those around us that we are strong, open, and available.

You be the judge: When you see someone walking towards you with folded arms and hung head, do you perceive confidence in that person? Do you trust that person? When you find yourself in a bad mood you can't get yourself out of, are you likely to have a superhero's posture or to fall into the cool kid slump? One thing is for sure: If we are folding our arms or hunching over to create the kind of protective posture that shields our hearts from others, we are inhibiting the healing power of our breath, and the science backing mindful breathing is not easy to argue with.

If we subconsciously arrange our bodies in unhealthy postures when feeling sad, angry, or anxious, perhaps we are capable of creating a healthier internal landscape by consciously shifting into healthy posture. I believe that this is another instinctive practice that has been lost by many modern men and women. If we return to our roots by strengthening our mind-body connection through mindfulness practice, we will reclaim our innate agency over ailments like chronic pain. If we continue disengaging into comfort created by screens and furniture, we are severing the connection between our body and mind, suppressing our natural capability for self-healing.

We see this phenomenon all around us as "body language." Watching others we see pictures painted by their bodies of what is happening on the inside. Through our ancient instincts, we decode this body language into our perception of others, trying to get a handle on their otherwise hidden inner experience. We then utilize these perceptions to decide whether to tend and befriend them or to keep our distance. This is why body language plays a large role in how successful we are socially.

Research indicates that bigger, more confident body shapes (sometimes called "power poses") encourage feelings

Power posing is the practice of making the body bigger to create feelings of power. Power poses send a signal from body to mind (and to those around us) that we are strong, confident, and capable. Performing these postures when we are nervous can help us generate the internal power we need to overcome feelings of weakness.

of power and emotional ease, improve testosterone production, and decrease cortisol production.[3] Inward or guarded shapes (protective postures) encourage feelings of fear, anxiety, and a lack of self-confidence and ramp up cortisol and adrenaline production. By power posing for just five minutes before an interview or first date, you are more likely to communicate that you are capable and desirable even if you are secretly terrified on the inside. If the way we choose to shape our body can make us more successful, can it also help us heal from chronic pain? Try the embodiment practice below to witness the power of smiling with your entire body. For more embodiment practices, visit the *Burn Your Chair* bonus resource guide at *www.burnyourchair.com*.

Practice—Be Bigger

1. Find a shape you could hold for a few minutes of centering. Create a mind-body connection by becoming aware of your resting breath pattern.
2. Notice the shape you've chosen and how it feels. Now intentionally begin to deepen your breath, encouraging the inhales to become fuller and the exhales to become longer.
3. Aided by your deepening breath, broaden and lengthen your body. If you're sitting down or standing, roll your shoulders back, push your chest forward and lengthen your spine. If you're lying down, make a star shape with your body. Absorb as much space in the room as you can.
4. Check back in with your body. What do you notice? Is it easier or harder to maintain deep breathing in your adjusted posture? Does it feel easy or challenging to maintain this large shape? What happens within your mind as you practice being bigger?

Reshaping Our Embodiment

The reason we are more attracted to others who display positive body language is because we know intuitively through the instinct of basic human empathy that this is an expression of their inner health. When we see someone burying their heart under folded arms, protecting their neck with shrugged shoulders, or constantly looking down at the ground to avoid eye contact, we know intuitively that they are displaying protective mechanisms they have established in order to shield themselves from life. This phenomenon is known as *embodiment*, the physical manifestation of our emotional and psychological state.

Embodiment can express our anxiety or our pleasure, our anger or our joy. It can be expressed through tone of voice, facial expressions, the clothes we choose to wear, and the way we shape our posture. Some forms of embodiment occur on a deeper level and are not visible to the naked eye. For instance, in response to chronic stress many people breathe very shallow, a form of embodiment that is easy to hide but creates many problems. Some invisible types of embodiment occur so much deeper that not even the individual can perceive the toxicity brewing within themselves without some kind of self-awareness encouraging practice.

The protective postures we maintain in order to shield ourselves from life and suppress our inner experience have devastating impacts on our health. The compression of our organs and muscles and the suppression of our breath starves our cells of oxygen, leading to chronic conditions like TMS and exacerbation of stress, anxiety, and depression. Ironically, these postures were subconsciously created to protect the mind from dealing with the myriad of emotions constantly churning within us, yet they simultaneously wreak havoc on our bodies which in turn redirects pain to the mind. Since the body and mind are constantly communicating, the temporary protection provided by these shapes leads to long-term physical and psychological problems. Taking these shapes is like covering a gaping wound with a bandage without stopping the bleeding or cleansing the infection.

What's fascinating is that when we modify the parts of ourselves which chronically maintain unhealthy embodiment by consciously reshaping ourselves, the emotions we were hiding from (or were hidden from us) have a tendency to resurface. This is why Kate felt a flood of emotion when she reshaped her embodiment from a protective posture to an open one. When we change from a protective shape to an open shape, we mentally touch upon the physical parts of us that need our attention, and in turn we're likely to be greeted by the emotions we were protecting ourselves from. Some readers may actually experience great sadness when they try the smiling practice offered previously. This isn't because there's something wrong with them; it's because they haven't allowed themselves to consciously smile in so long that a smile acts as a doorway for trapped emotions to come out of.

There are many ways to reshape our embodiment. Within the physical form, embodiment can be reshaped by contrasting our habitual tension patterns and protective postures with active rest. Within the mental, emotional, and spiritual bodies, embodiment can be reshaped through practices like mindful breathing and meditation to contrast toxic thought patterns with healthy self-focus and awareness.

Through consistent practice of the interventions that best suit an individual's unique needs, habitual tension and toxic thought patterns displayed through embodiment can be modified and eliminated. Simply put, by changing our shape or shifting our focus, we

Expressing oneself through exercise and hobbies allows tension and energy to be released. Regularly releasing our excess energy is a vital part of living a pain-free life.

encourage natural healing from the things that bind us. By opening our bodies, we open our emotional baggage. We create the conditions needed to sort through the things we hold onto in order to release the things that no longer serve us so that we can live lives free from pain.

In addition to the practices of active rest, mindful breathing, and biofeedback, we can utilize many forms of therapeutic exercise to reshape our embodiment. Expressing oneself through dancing, running, swimming, lifting weights, making love, making music or any of the millions of other cathartic forms of physical and mental energy release available within the human body helps to expel the tension we would otherwise hold onto and transform into pain. By expressing our feelings rather than repressing them, we create an internal landscape that is spacious, inviting, and serene, which allows the innate process of self-healing to occur as nature intended.

The Eight Essential Healing Postures

If we move more, we suffer less pain and disease. In an era dominated by one shape (the chair shape), humans are moving less and less. The most common prescription for the sitting disease is exercise, but it is proving to be an incomplete solution. Instead of sitting all day and moving for an hour in the gym, we need to find a gentle baseline of movement throughout the day. This movement can be found during our sedentary hours by the combination of active rest and posture cycling. If we shift periodically through ergonomic human shapes when at rest rather than remain in one shape all day, we can live lives free from pain.

Part Two—The Eight Essential Healing Postures

You were born with a set of invisible tools, tools that when rediscovered will allow you to heal the parts of you that hurt. These tools mend simultaneously the physical, emotional, and mental parts of you that are linked to pain and disease. In order to employ them, you will need to revert to a more instinctive way of living. You will have to reject the societal norms that hurt you, and practice putting yourself first. In this part of the book I will encourage you to do things that may seem radical. Things that are sure to make you and others around you uncomfortable. However, if you are willing to be uncomfortable temporarily, the benefits will be tremendous.

Burn your chair. Get out of your seat and onto the floor. If a part of you is aching, tired, or tight, do something about it. Does sitting at your desk leave you hunched forward and stiff? Stand up, take a walk, and straighten yourself out. Are long hours in front of the TV or computer making you feel lonely or depressed? Go for a walk in nature to reconnect with your roots. Do you notice tension or anxiety as you stand in line at the coffee shop? Place your hands on your hips, and make your body bigger to reshape your embodiment. Every cat and dog stretches when they've been still for too long, shouldn't you? We are so accustomed to accepting the seats and shapes of our daily lives, suffering in them as if we have no choice.

The practices offered in this book will not align with the norms of modern society because they directly oppose each other. The formalities of our culture force us into deforming postures that trap our bodies and numb our emotions. Active rest offers instead a path that reconnects you to yourself in the present moment, alleviating body and mind. To attain these benefits you will have to become a part of the counterculture that refuses to sit down and accept pain as the status quo.

Each of the following chapters focuses on one of the eight postures I consider to be essential for encouraging self-healing within the human body. The postures have been paired with **counter postures**, positions that are useful to shift into after holding the initial shape. Pairing postures with their counter positions ensures that time spent in one shape does not create dysfunction in another part of the body. It is also possible to receive a similar effect by simply returning to a neutral position and breathing deeply for a few moments.

You'll also find suggestions for a daily goal of time spent within each pose at the beginning of each chapter. These suggestions are not etched in stone. They're just signposts pointing you in the direction of self-discovering an amount of time that is right for you. In fact, I consider most of the times offered to be generous minimums. Your needs will be different day-to-day; therefore, the amount of time spent in each pose should vary in response. Keep the suggestions in mind as you start practicing, but listen to your body first. The signals of your body will offer the most accurate measure of whether you need to push yourself to stay in a little longer for added benefits or if the shape is no longer useful.

It's not necessary to try and do every pose every day; however, this would provide you with a very complete daily posture practice. Postures can be performed completely independent from each other and spaced out throughout your day, or they could be performed all together in one long posture cycling practice to create a movement routine. Practice first thing in the morning to refresh or before bed to calm. Focus on the postures that speak to you on any given day for relieving acute pain, or practice them all regularly to maintain a more consistent and global sense of ease within you. I suggest the latter whenever possible. For more variations of the shapes and strategies for implementing the practices in daily life, visit the bonus resource guide at *www.burnyourchair.com*.

If you feel some of these postures are unavailable to you, don't give up. Proceed in your practice with cautious curiosity. Be playful. Be creative. All of these postures have room for self-expression. They may require small modifications and support that help you feel safe. Or they may require complete reconstruction, resulting in a shape that is only partially inspired by the original offering. Look at the illustrations in each chapter to inspire ideas of how to modify the shapes for your needs, but don't worry about looking like the people in the pictures. Rather, mimic the shape demonstrated much like a child would, seeking a similar but not exact version of the shape guided by the sensations of your body. Your body will tell you how to adjust in order to stay safe. Consistent attempts at this practice will gradually transform your body and change what you are capable of.

Mindful self-exploration will address your unique body better than any ancient text or movement system could ever hope to. After enough consistent practice, you might discover yourself instinctively assuming these postures without consciously intending to, guided by the edges of your body and mind. This will be the moment in which your innate ability to self-heal is fully restored. The only teacher you will need from then on will be the one guiding you from within.

5

Sitting on the Ground (Sukasana/Agura)

"If you fall, I'll be there."—The Ground

Benefits: *Improved Posture, Reduced Aches and Pains, Better Digestion, Increased Strength and Flexibility, Improved Circulation, Extended Longevity, Improved Attention and Productivity*
Counter Positions: *Standing and Walking, Sphinx*
Daily Goal: *Ten Minutes or More*

The simplest way to relieve oneself from the burden of chronic pain is to push furniture aside and sit on the ground. By sitting on the ground, we remove the items that decrease the need for our body and mind to remain connected. This body-mind connection is the key to unlocking the benefits of active rest. Combined with mindful breathing, the practice of finding active rest by sitting on the ground provides us innumerable health benefits, ranging from improved posture to extended lifespan.

When you sit on the ground, your body is encouraged to maintain a healthy level of mental and muscular engagement. It affords you the freedom to periodically change your sitting position, whereas sitting in a plush office chair, recliner, or sofa encourages you to fully disengage and remain immobilized for hours. According to a recent article published in *The International Journal of Sports Physical Therapy*, sitting disengaged for long periods of time weakens and atrophies our glute muscles.[1] This eventually leads to *gluteal inhibition*, a condition more affectionately known as "dead butt syndrome." Dead butt syndrome is a proponent of back pain, warped posture, reduced athletic performance, and trouble balancing. Once we have a dead butt, it doesn't simply wake up like a sleeping limb when we finally stand up. Instead our glutes can remain disengaged semi-permanently and lead to a whole host of painful dysfunctions that affect our quality of life.

Sitting on the ground frees the body from the confines of chairs. Free to move, you'll discover many variations to sitting that make it something you can do for long periods of time without pain.

There are many exercises you can perform to reactivate your glutes, such as the pelvic tilt exercise offered in Chapter 1. However, this problem can be circumnavigated by simply changing how you sit, where you sit, and how often you posture cycle. The engagement that is necessary to sit on the floor in proper pelvic alignment inherently requires a gentle level of glute and core engagement which prevents these muscles from turning off. Sitting in this way improves our strength and flexibility, affording more mobility to the spine, hips and knees. By keeping our muscles activated, sitting on the ground also generates a greater baseline level of body awareness. This heightened body awareness combined with the freedom of not having to conform to the shape of a chair allows us to respond appropriately when we feel sore or tired by shifting our position or getting up to move. Put simply, from the ground we're more likely to listen to the signals our body is sending us, and we have the freedom to respond easily.

Increasing body awareness is crucial in further developing the practice of biofeedback, our greatest ally in improving posture and living a life free from pain. Rolling the shoulders away from the ears; shifting side to side to change the cross of our legs; tipping the pelvis forward to lengthen the low back; or changing our position completely are all examples of biofeedback reactions that make sitting on the ground more doable, which also keep the body at a higher baseline level of activation.

Evidence suggests that the light activity of periodically shifting our posture while sitting on the ground combined with proper postural alignment improves the circulation of our blood. When we sit in a chair, the distance from the feet to the heart is much greater than when sitting on the ground. This makes it more challenging for the deoxygenated blood in our legs to recirculate to the heart, as it fights a longer path resisted by gravity and more tightly closed off venous valves. A 2006 study conducted at Waseda University compared the sitting practices of Eastern and Western cultures. In particular the researchers noted the difference in hemodynamics (movement of blood through the body) while sitting on the ground versus sitting in a chair. This cross-cultural examination discovered that sitting on the ground not only improved the alignment of the musculoskeletal system but in turn aligned the circulatory system, reducing the risk of developing conditions

Elevating your hips from the ground while seated will make more sitting positions available. To come into "stacked logs pose," cross one leg over the other, placing the ankle (not the foot) on the thigh right above the knee. This is an intense hip stretch for many people, but a bolster or other support under the hips will make the position more sustainable.

such as deep vein thrombosis and chronic leg edema from long periods of sitting in a chair.[2]

This improved blood circulation may explain why sitting on the ground while eating is considered a practice of better health in some cultures. In ancient Ayurvedic medicine (a sister science to yoga), sitting on the ground to eat is believed to improve digestion and aid in weight loss. An easeful flow of blood encourages the organs to function properly and delivers the nutrients released from food to the tissues. Improved blood flow may also play a part in helping to release stomach acid and enzymes that aid in the breakdown of food. The core engagement necessary for sitting on the ground may also lend a hand in digestion. Leaning forward over crossed legs with each bite puts gentle pressure on the abdomen. All this shifting around as we sit on the floor encourages *peristalsis*, the milking action of the digestive tract that squeezes food to break it down and encourage it to travel onward to the next organ. The gentle activity of eating in this way may also encourage a slightly higher metabolism, which could support the weight loss idea.

Growing up I was encouraged to be a part of the "clean plate club." Not finishing a meal was wasteful and could be considered an insult to the chef. When I started sitting on the ground to eat, I soon noticed that the portion sizes I was accustomed to were impossible to finish. Leaning forward over crossed legs puts just enough pressure on the abdomen to initiate stop signals from the stomach sooner than when sitting in a chair. In a chair, we can just lean back and push our belly forward to make more room for food we don't really need.

Sitting on the ground unlocks many new possibilities in our bodies and minds and may be one of the keys for maximizing human potential. A 2018 study published in *Science Daily* by San Francisco State University asked college students to perform math problems while slumped over in their chairs and then to repeat similar problems while sitting up straight or standing. Over half of the students reported that having healthy posture helped them to focus and solve the problems with greater accuracy.[3] It seems that when the body slacks off, the mind follows, whereas utilizing an empowered position optimizes our ability to focus.

The act of sitting on the ground isn't the only part of this practice that improves our health. Getting up from the ground is now being linked to an increase in our life expectancy. In 2012, a study published in the *European Journal of Preventive Cardiology* found that being able to stand up from the ground without holding onto anything correlates with improved longevity. To get up from the ground without using your hands requires a combination of strength, flexibility, balance, and coordination that are all essential parts of our autonomy, a vital condition of living a long and pain-free life.[4]

Sitting on the ground requires more effort than sitting in a chair, hence the "active" in active rest. However, there's no need to be masochistic. This should be a practice of self-love, not a contest to see who can sit on the ground the longest. A firm pillow combined with our own engagement can effectively replace the support from the chairs that we are accustomed to. A wall or an ottoman can become the perfect back

rest when our core grows weary from supporting us. The idea is not to seek out painful ways of resting in order to heal, but rather to find what level of discomfort we can endure if we know it is doing us some good. The key here is to recognize the difference between sharp, harmful pain and therapeutic discomfort.

The problem many will face, especially after years of sitting in chairs, is that sitting cross-legged on the floor simply isn't possible due to tightness in the hips, knees, and back, as well as weakness in the core. This is why it is important to explore each of the eight postures with patience. Seek out what is

"Ninety-ninety pose" is an excellent shape for building hip mobility and improving posture. From a cross-legged position, bend one leg behind you, aiming for 90-degree angles at both knees. For a gentler shape, narrow the distance between the legs, decrease the knee angles, or boost the hips.

available in your body *right now*. Don't worry about how you look or what you think you should be able to do. Instead, pay attention to how you feel, and notice how you can support yourself to feel better. Sitting with legs outstretched may make this position more appropriate for your body. Or perhaps sitting on a bolster or step so that the hips are above the legs will make crossing the legs possible.

In order to ensure sitting on the ground is a fruitful practice in your body, you must remain mindful. The most important mindfulness practice while sitting on the ground is to keep checking in with your foundation, the tilt of your pelvis. If you are low on energy and maintaining an anterior pelvic tilt feels impossible, consider sitting with your back against a wall. Lift your seat for a moment, align your pelvis in a healthy tilt, and then wedge your tail in-between the floor and wall for support. If a wall is unavailable, place your hands behind you and focus on pushing your hips and chest forward with each breath.

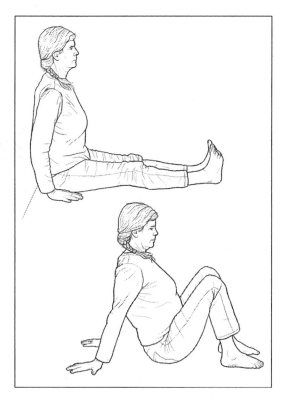

Supporting the back by leaning against a wall or something similar is a great way to give the postural muscles a break when sitting on the ground. In lieu of a wall, place your hands behind you. The second shape offers an excellent upper body stretch.

Each time you realize that a position is becoming uncomfortable, explore the little changes that make it more manageable. Eventually the position you are in will no longer be sustainable, as your glutes may begin to tire or your knees may begin to say "enough!"

5. Sitting on the Ground (Sukasana/Agura)

This is the perfect time to explore one of the seven other essential healing postures, including but not limited to the counter positions offered above.

There's a Time and Place

Although I label these postures essential and have encouraged you to avoid prolonged periods of sitting on furniture, it is important to recognize that there are many situations in which sitting in a chair may be the best thing for your body. By saying, *"Burn Your Chair"* I am not encouraging you to be unkind to yourself or to overuse active rest postures just as we have the tendency to overuse furniture.

A few years ago my partner Mali and I spent a month in Italy, work-trading for a place to stay while writing and exploring. One weekend we took a break from work and headed to Rome to visit the Colosseum, The Pantheon, and Vatican City to soak up some culture. We walked for hours in the blistering summer heat on unforgiving cobblestone streets. My bad hip acted up, and my knees were reminding me of their multiple surgeries. Periodically I practiced my active rest postures (squatting with my back against a wall like a smart tourist).They helped me endure, but I wasn't eating or drinking enough water, and soon I was completely exhausted.

We finally made it to a restaurant for a late lunch. Up until this moment, whenever I went out to eat, I always wished that more restaurants offered the opportunity to sit on the ground to eat like some sushi places. But as I sat down on a rickety old wooden chair underneath an umbrella in front of a centuries-old building in Rome, I was so thankful to have a chair to sit on. I knew that I didn't have the energy to support myself in an active seat and that I needed to dedicate all of my reserves towards hydrating and nourishing my body. At that moment, the chair was a technology I gladly embraced. This reminded me that there is a time and place for everything and that no practice or technology should be overused or abolished.

My partner and I were so tired and hungry that we stayed at the restaurant for hours. We ate plate after plate, drank a few liters of wine, and contemplated dessert. Gradually my glutes began to hurt from hours of being squashed. My back and shoulders couldn't seem to find comfortable positions. My body was telling me it was time to get up.

In just one day I saw the cycles of work, active rest, and passive rest that are essential to human life. I realized this idea that I wanted to share with the world about active rest was not a complete answer to the sedentary living epidemic. The answer is not simply to burn our chairs. We need to develop the inner awareness necessary to effectively balance work, rest, play, and totally letting go in a way that is healthy, sustainable, and feeds our soul. Too bad that message couldn't be boiled down into a catchy title.

Practice—Sitting on the Ground

1. Find a firm pillow, bolster, or folded-up blanket that is of adequate thickness to boost your seat far enough off the ground so that you can cross your legs. If crossing your legs causes you sharp pain no matter the amount of lift, extend your legs out straight instead. If it feels safe to sit cross-legged without much support, do so, perhaps adding support once you begin to fatigue.

2. For a more restful posture, lean your back against a wall or another supportive part of your environment. This may be the only variation you are capable of at first if your posture is very poor or your body is very tight. Don't worry, this is sure to change over time with consistent practice. For a more active and strengthening seat, sit without any additional support, utilizing core engagement to keep from rounding your back.

3. Tip your pelvis forward to lengthen your low back. Roll your shoulders back, and push your chest forward to create space for deeper breathing. Lengthen your neck by slightly tucking your chin and pushing the crown of the head upwards.

4. Over the course of your sitting practice, use each inhale to help you sit up taller. Recall the image offered in the three-part breath practice. Imagine a string is attached to the top of your head and is pulling you taller with each breath. With

5. Sitting on the Ground (Sukasana/Agura)

The key to sitting on the ground is periodic posture cycling. Change your shape often to get the most out of your practice. Experiment with how you arrange your legs and how you support yourself. Over time you will discover the positions you like as well as the positions you don't like (but know you need in order to heal).

each exhale, gently engage your core to maintain the length you've created.

5. Set a goal for an amount of time or a certain number of tasks to do from this position, aiming for ten or more minutes sitting on the ground each day. More benefits will be gained from this practice if done in mediation because you can focus on posture and breath entirely. However, it will still be beneficial when used as a seat for work, rest, or play. Over the course of your practice, pay attention to the signals your body is sending you. If one knee is saying, "I don't like this anymore!" change the cross in your legs, and see if that helps. If your glutes are feeling compressed, try sitting more towards the front of your support cushion, encouraging more of your weight to land on your sitz bones. You can find more ground-sitting variations in the *Burn Your Chair* bonus resource guide at *www.burnyourchair.com*. If no change in your seat or rearrangement of your legs offers you relief, try on one of the other seven essential healing postures.

6

Sphinx (Salamba Bhujangasana/Sufinkusu)

"If you would seek health, look first to the spine."
—Socrates

Benefits: Strengthens Postural Muscles, Stabilizes Shoulders, Improves Spinal Extension, Decompresses the Spine, Lengthens the Abdomen, Activates Upper Back, Soothes Lower Back, Improves Circulation in the Legs, Relaxes Pelvic Floor Muscles, Improves Gut Health
Counter Position: Kneeling, Hanging
Daily Goal: Five Minutes or More

When seeking to restore our body's natural ability to self-heal, we must continue to examine the differences between the way we live our modern lives and the way our ancestors and pain-free contemporaries live. The difference isn't long hours of being sedentary, as demonstrated by the millions of people who work sedentary professions who do not report chronic pain. It's not even the chair that's the problem. It's that we have made all of our positions chair shaped. We are not mindful of our edges and therefore do not respond to the needs of our body when it has been in one shape too long. We don't cycle through healthy doses of movement or counter positions to return our bodies to neutral after long periods of time in one position. As cited in Chapter 2, even after discovering the usefulness of chairs and stools, pain-free people will not choose a seated position for all activities. Instead, they cycle through a few of the hundreds of other positions the human body is capable of. This allows them to more easily complete their task and to reset themselves from the effects of the

6. Sphinx (Salamba Bhujangasana/Sufinkusu)

shapes they hold more regularly.

If you are tired from sitting upright on the ground, your low back is feeling tight or your upper back is rounding, roll onto your belly and place your forearms on the floor below your shoulders. Actively push your forearms into the floor, and allow your spine to extend. This gentle backbend will offer your body healthy stressors that are opposite that of the sitting

Like sitting on the ground, sphinx pose is an instinctive shape that children move into naturally.

shape. The front of the body will open, gently stretching weary and compressed core muscles. Sphinx is a great position for reading, watching TV, or working on your laptop. If you watch children, you will see them naturally assume sphinx pose as an active place to play and rest. Many of our mammalian brethren such as dogs and cats rest in sphinx pose. This body shape was clearly regarded by our ancestors as a regal posture, one that summons strength and pride, as demonstrated by the Great Sphinx of Giza who watches over the catacombs of ancient Egypt.

Whether we are talking about sitting on the ground or sitting in a chair, sitting is a position of flexion, meaning the joint angles are decreased. Extension is the opposite of flexion. Sphinx pose takes all the joints that are flexed while seated into extension and flexes the one joint that is not flexed while seated: the shoulders. This allows the shoulders to be strengthened in a way that they cannot be while seated. In sphinx the legs are free to be long and loose without any pressure placed on them from the weight of the body, like when seated or standing. This allows blood to circulate into and out of the legs more freely without much resistance from gravity on its path to and from the heart.

95

The sphinx shape was regarded by our ancestors as a position of power and protection.

Just as the pelvis is the foundation for sitting or standing, the shoulders become the foundation in sphinx pose. This gives the hip and core muscles a much needed break. While the hip and core muscles rest, the shoulders are offered an opportunity to strengthen. The postural muscles of the upper back and neck are engaged to hold this shape. This reactivates muscle fibers that are typically less active and may have been dormant or weakened by overstretching while seated. The muscles between the shoulder blades are asked to retract in order to maintain healthy alignment sphinx pose, which makes them stronger. Stronger upper body muscles will be more active while assuming sitting and standing postures, helping to protect the body from the woes of the cool kid slump and aiding back-saving biofeedback.

Imagine the spine as a spring. While we sit and stand throughout our day, gravity is compressing us from head to toe. In upright positions the coils of the spring (our joints) are being pressed towards one another. Unlike a spring we have tissues, organs, and nerves that lie between our coils, all of which benefit greatly from spaciousness. When lying in sphinx, the front of the body naturally decompresses through extension of the spine. This extension can slightly compress the low back if the posture is not performed properly, but an active sphinx shape offers us a vector for creating spinal traction. For a step-by-step description of how to properly practice sphinx pose in order to avoid low back compression and encourage spinal traction, see the practice at the end of the chapter.

Another little-known benefit of sphinx pose is how it encourages us to relax our pelvic floor muscles. Being able to relax the pelvic floor is vital to our health. A chronically tense pelvic floor can lead to problems like constipation, pain when passing waste, incomplete emptying of waste, bladder pain, incontinence, and sexual dysfunction. As the abdominal muscles are lengthened and relaxed in sphinx pose, their fascial connections to pelvic floor muscles also relax. The pressure of the pubis against the ground doubles this effect, and mindful breathing into the pelvic floor increases the benefits further.

As is true for all of the eight essential healing postures, mindful breathing is the key to achieving maximum benefits from sphinx pose. We can use mindfulness to direct the air pressure created by inhaling into the parts of us that need additional stretching. As we exhale, we can direct the relaxation that naturally occurs while breathing out to the parts of us that need to let go. This allows us to self-massage our tissues and organs through the rising and falling of air pressure within us.

In sphinx pose, the pressure of the gut against the ground combined with the rising and falling of the breath naturally massages the digestive organs. The pressure on the gut is increased during the inhale and decreased on the exhale. The benefits to our digestive system found in sphinx are twice as effective as sitting on the ground because of the additional pressure placed on the gut from our body weight combined with the stretching of the abdomen.

When beginning to practice sphinx, think of the sensations you feel within it as healthy doses of oppositional stressors to those found while seated. After long periods in sphinx pose, your forearms may become sore from the pressure placed on them, your shoulders and postural muscles may become weary, and your neck may want to disengage to drop the weight of the head. This is the perfect time to cycle into a counterpose or to lie all the way down with your arms alongside your body and one cheek to the ground.

Common problems you may experience in sphinx are weakness in the shoulders, a tight low back, or issues being belly down (such as pregnancy and obesity). Common modifications are to elevate

Sphinx is the perfect counterpose for long periods of sitting in chairs or on the ground. It changes the base of our posture from hips to shoulders, allowing the legs to decompress. It gently extends the spine and stretches the abdomen.

the forearms or pelvis (or both) with a bolster or pillow. Not all of these postures may be appropriate for you at any given time. However, there are often modifications that will make the positions more available. If you are willing to experiment, you will most likely find a version of each of the eight essential healing postures that you enjoy.

Case Study—Janet

A longtime client of mine, Janet, has struggled for most of her adult life with chronic back and hip pain. At 76, she has had multiple surgeries to address her compacted hip sockets and thoracic kyphosis (forward rounding of the upper back). The forward rounding of her upper back and subsequent tightness in her abdomen leave her feeling chronically out of breath. Janet has a very low pain tolerance, likely due to an overstressed nervous system that is always on high alert from constant irritation. This makes exercise very uncomfortable for her, and she has a tough time delineating between pain and therapeutic discomfort. She also suffers stress-induced urinary incontinence and other disorders associated with voluntary control of pelvic floor muscles.

A widow of ten years, Janet keeps herself going by continuing to work as a teacher in a public school. It goes without saying that being

6. Sphinx (Salamba Bhujangasana/Sufinkusu)

a teacher is one of the most important jobs we have in our society today. What often goes overlooked is the fact that teachers are asked to completely sacrifice their own well-being in order to promote children's well-being and learning outcomes. This societal request for self-sacrifice combined with low levels of self-awareness led Janet to develop the host of symptoms she suffered from.

Janet, like many teachers, has to stand and sit for long periods of time. Her hip pain and sciatica comes from chronically compressed hip joints. Her thoracic kyphosis likely formed over time from a hardening of the habitual shape of slumping over a desk grading papers or leaning forward to look over a child's shoulder as they worked. Periodically she would notice herself leaking small amounts of urine when coughing, sneezing, or raising her voice, a symptom of a chronically stressed and weakened pelvic floor. Janet attributed this problem to long periods of holding her bladder full, as teachers aren't allowed to leave the classroom unattended for bathroom breaks. Her lack of self-care culminated into a very painful existence. In combination with other lifestyle factors such as poor nutrition and inadequate rest, the cycle of pain, dysfunction, and self-sacrifice was well set. Janet didn't try to hurt herself. She was simply following the norms of our culture and demands of her profession.

Janet's high sensitivity to pain meant her initial sessions with me were focused mainly on calming her nervous system through mindful breathing and gentle assisted stretches. Whenever I asked her to perform movements on her own, she could only produce a very small range of motion, so small that some of the movements were imperceptible, and I would have to ask her if she understood the exercise. "Yes, but I can't seem to get my body to do that," she'd say. I helped her to achieve greater ranges of motion simply by offering reassurances that the movements were safe and that her body was capable.

At some point in each session, when I would coach her to an edge, Janet would stop moving or leave the posture completely, grimacing and complaining of pain. We talked at great length about the difference between sharp pain and therapeutic discomfort, but when asked to delineate between the two, Janet would often repeat, "No, this is pain." Yet when taken to similar or even more intense body positions through assisted stretching, Janet was able to breathe through the discomfort and stay with her edges considerably longer.

I gave Janet a program of movements and stretches to perform on her own in addition to her once weekly session. When asked, Janet was honest; she almost never did her program. When she did, she could only get through the warm-ups. I tried motivating her to get moving by offering the idea that there's no way she could be the best version of herself if she was in constant pain and was therefore doing a disservice to the children she served by not focusing on self-care. While she appreciated my strategy, this extrinsic motivation did not produce any positive effects.

When we did find movements that Janet felt comfortable with and was motivated to repeat, I encouraged her to focus on those and not to worry too much about completing her entire program. I didn't want her to fall into the trap of "all-or-nothing" thinking because moving with me for an hour a week just wasn't enough. She needed to move every day and to move with intention. If we hoped to effect real change together, we needed to keep working to discover movements and postures she felt empowered to perform on her own. We started to have some success in combining repetition of the movements she enjoyed with small doses of gently approaching the edge. Just as we began to turn the corner with this new way of practicing together, the COVID-19 pandemic hit. My thriving yoga therapy practice, only a year old at the time, had to shut down in-person operations for the foreseeable future as a nonessential business.

I was devastated, but I knew I needed to look at the pandemic as an opportunity to evolve. I decided to shift all of my classes and sessions online. I encouraged my students and clients to try and do the same, to look at the changes forced upon them as reasons to reinvent themselves. My online classes were immediately successful because everyone was in need of new ways to de-stress. Sadly, Janet did not feel seen in group classes, as the global cues were not enough to safely address the extremeness of her experience. Like many of my private clients, Janet was initially uninterested in online private sessions since she already spent so many hours on the computer teaching. I feared Janet would lose touch with her practice and lose the progress she had gained.

COVID meant teachers around the world faced great uncertainty and anxiety about the security of their career. Schools went back and forth between remote, in-person, and hybrid models in an attempt to slow the spread of the virus. Now in her golden years, Janet had to completely relearn the one thing she was best at: teaching. She faced the fervor of frustrated students she needed to reeducate in a techno-assisted environment that she knew little of. On top of this, she was having to manage her own fears of a world where life-threatening disease was lurking around every corner.

I thought for sure the massive amount of screen time required of her as a teacher combined with the communal anxiety of the pandemic would exacerbate her pain significantly. Yet Janet chose to transform. Something inside her shifted as society underwent global change. Eventually she reached out to me to reconnect for online sessions. At first I was a little nervous that we would encounter her previous problems with movement. Without being physically there to protect and encourage her, I worried I had no way of helping her to continue growing.

In our initial online session, I was awe inspired by what I saw. As I invited Janet to close her eyes and focus on her breathing, I saw her ability to self-heal firsthand. Janet took a big inhale, and with a look of gentle effort on her face, she straightened her posture dramatically. Her thoracic kyphosis completely disappeared right before my eyes! I was shocked and elated to see the fruits of her self-care practice. I couldn't believe how much Janet had progressed in the short time we had been apart. I was truly stunned, but I decided to share my excitement with her at the end of the session so I could see more.

I led her through a review of movements she had attempted in previous sessions. Janet demonstrated control and awareness of her body that I didn't know she was capable of. There were still noticeable limitations, of course, but something was different. As she approached more intense edges, her posture would almost completely disengage to protect the weak link she was working on. Yet I noticed a willingness to be within discomfort that I never witnessed in her before. I was so touched by her transformation that tears glazed my eyes.

At the end of her session, I asked Janet what she attributed the change in her practice to. "Well, when I realized I would be on my own all the time, I knew I had to see it as an opportunity to take care of myself or I'd really be in trouble," she said with a look of hopeful sadness. "My first day teaching online was unbearable. The children are very hard to manage over the internet. I was so frustrated I wanted to scream!" she said with a look of disgust on her face. "I was so tense and sore. I thought about what you said about not sitting in a chair all day, so that night I didn't sit in my recliner. I sat on the floor. But I couldn't stay there very long because it was very uncomfortable for my hips."

"I discovered that recreating the pose from our last in-person session—lying on my belly with a pillow under my chest—was a position I could hold much longer than sitting," she continued. "After lying like that for a few minutes each night before bed, I feel like I can finally breathe again, and I sleep like I haven't in years."

Through her self-practice, Janet had discovered the shape that she needed most for supporting the transformation of her body. She found a posture that was the opposite of the slumped sitting and standing postures she had relied on for decades to facilitate her work. Armed with the ancient shape of the sphinx, Janet was able to transform her posture, both by gently extending and tractioning her spine for long periods of time and by strengthening the muscles in her upper back. This newfound strength and flexibility allows her to take on an entirely new shape when she is being self-aware, a skill she is still working on solidifying through daily practice.

Janet no longer experiences chronic shortness of breath, and when she does acutely, she reports that sphinx pose aids her in recollecting her breathing. She also finds the position relieving for her legs, hips, and back after long periods of sitting in a chair, something she now tries to limit as much as possible. When asked about her incontinence, Janet said, "I haven't even thought about it lately. But no, I can't remember the last time it happened." Perhaps relaxing her abdomen by regularly practicing sphinx pose aided in her relief.

It would be foolhardy to assume that Janet's transformation came from one shape. Surely the ability to take regular bathroom breaks for the first time in decades played a larger role in relieving her incontinence than sphinx pose. But without her newfound self-awareness, she would not have listened to her body's signals regardless of where she was. All it took was a little more focus on herself to quicken her stride on the path of self-healing. Janet's story

6. Sphinx (Salamba Bhujangasana/Sufinkusu)

is a wonderful example of our body's ability to transform when nurtured by our attention and the practice of self-care.

Practice—Sphinx

1. Lie on the ground belly down and place your forearms flat. Position the elbows directly below your shoulders. If you find undue discomfort in the forearms, elbows, or hips, use pillows, blankets, or another anti-fatigue surface (like a yoga mat) to create a greater sense of comfort in these areas.
2. As you inhale, push your elbows and forearms down into the ground, and lengthen your neck to lift your head higher.
3. As you exhale, draw your shoulder blades together, and push your chest forward by energetically pulling your elbows back. This will create a traction effect within your spine. Imagine

Experiment with various arrangements of your arms and legs to create different sensations in sphinx. Pad the arms or boost the chest with a pillow or blanket to make the position less fatiguing.

pulling your chest away from your hips while keeping the hips rooted.

4. Once you feel comfortable with the combination of the subtle shoulder movements and the pattern of your breath, add in the practice of directional breathing. Send your breath to the parts of you that need attention. If your aim is to relax your pelvic floor, initiate the inhales by directing the air downwards towards the pelvis. If you want to receive more of a gut massage, instead send the in-breath into the belly, swelling it down towards the floor. Experiment with where you can direct your breath for addressing the unique needs of your body.

For more sphinx variations visit the *Burn Your Chair* bonus resource guide at *www.burnyourchair.com.*

7

Kneeling
(Vajrasana/Seiza)

"A lot of kneeling keeps one in good standing."
—Barbara Johnson

Benefits: *Improves Thigh/Knee/Ankle/Toe Flexibility, Improves Internal Rotation of the Hips, Reestablishes Arches in Flat Feet, Reduces Swelling of the Legs, Strengthens Core and Postural Muscles, Vital Link in Healthy Movement Patterns*
Counter Position: *Sphinx*
Daily Goal: *Three Minutes or More*

In many cultures, kneeling is seen as a respectful and attentive way to sit. In others, it is a place for devotional practice. In cultures undisturbed by technology, it is an essential posture for everyday life. In my body, kneeling can be quite excruciating (especially in the morning) as I have had four knee surgeries due to injuries from martial arts. After my fourth surgery, I had an intuition that spending more time kneeling would restore the health of my knees. I thought if I kept my knees flexible by kneeling regularly, I could escape the revolving door of Western medicine. My knee health has since improved dramatically. Now I wonder if I really needed all those surgeries or if I could have self-healed my knees aided by shapes like kneeling and a bit more patience with my body.

Every day for the past five years I have knelt despite the discomfort it causes. Sometimes I add a cushion between my calves and thighs or put a yoga block below my seat to lessen the intensity of the shape. Initially it seemed like resting in a full kneeling posture would simply never be available in my body again. But every day while assuming the kneeling position, tension released slowly but surely. Sometimes I notice internal "adjustments" of my knee tissues as I relax into the shape. Now I can kneel without support for long periods of time, and I can do things with my knees that I never thought would be possible.

Kneeling is an essential posture for healing because it improves the flexibility of the thigh muscles as well as the knee and ankle joints. It is an excellent shape for practicing tall posture and mindful breathing. The simple modification of tucking the toes lends itself to stretching the tissues of the feet, including the tough yet vulnerable plantar fascia. Keeping the plantar fascia supple is more important than most people realize. The posterior fascial chain extends from the soles of the feet up the back of our legs, up the entire backside of the body, over the back of the head, all the way to the eyebrows. If your feet are tight, there's a good chance other parts of your body that seem unrelated are suffering in suit.

By entering and exiting various kneeling postures multiple times a day, the foot muscles reestablish lost arches as they strengthen and stretch to meet the demands. Performing this action regularly and holding various kneeling shapes strengthen the quadriceps and anterior tibialis muscles. While kneeling we have a very stable postural base created by the length of the lower leg that's even more solid than some sitting or squatting postures. This stable base is an excellent place to work from and is the preferred meditation posture for many meditators around the world. For some people, the kneeling posture is more intuitive than sitting on the ground. This is because the main factor limiting postural alignment is the knees rather than the hips, making kneeling a nice place to rest from the demands of sitting and standing.

Kneeling is an instinctive shape that humans have been using for thousands of years to work, rest, and demonstrate devotion.

7. Kneeling (Vajrasana/Seiza)

Pregnant mothers, diabetics, and others who suffer from leg edema will find relief in kneeling, as the weight of the body helps to express trapped fluids from the legs. Laboring mothers also find relief in the kneeling posture since kneeling and squatting shapes have been shown by MRI scan studies to widen the pelvic outlet, explaining why these shapes facilitate less complicated births.[1] The kneeling position trains internal rotation of the hips, which is important for maintaining a healthy gait (walking/running movement pattern) and maximizing athletic performance. Without sufficient internal rotation of the hips, the knees and feet may cave inward to compensate. These compensations lead to injury and affect performance in athletic and nonathletic bodies alike. Most importantly, for all human bodies kneeling is a vital link that connects various functional movement patterns without which the body's potential is significantly stifled.

What I have learned from kneeling every day is that a willingness to be uncomfortable for short periods of time limits the accumulation of chronic pain in our body. Mindful doses of therapeutic discomfort can improve our resilience to injury and reintroduce freedom to our bodies. With patience, caution, and the courage to address our pain daily, we can heal the dysfunction in our bodies.

Now when I kneel, my thighs touch my calves without support, but I still feel attention-grabbing discomfort. The discomfort is loud enough to keep me present, yet the flexibility of my knees has changed enough so that I can tolerate kneeling for much longer than before. I protect my knees with a newfound awareness when running or sparring which has helped me to avoid reinjuring. My knees respond better to stress than they ever have before, even better than when I was in my 20s and first became dedicated to self-care.

There are many ways to modify the kneeling posture to meet your needs, but two deserve special mention. Try boosting up your seat with a block, stool, or cushion. In this variation, the prop should be small enough to fit between your legs without requiring an excessively wide straddle. Another option is to place a pillow or folded-up blanket between your calves and thighs. A nice way to rest intermittently while practicing kneeling is to lift the hips up and straighten the upper legs over the knees, sometimes called "knee standing." You can also experiment with "half kneeling" positions, where one leg is in a kneeling shape and the other is in a squatting shape. Be extra supportive when kneeling by placing pillows, blankets, or mats under your knees to pad the patellar (kneecap) tissues and surfaces. More kneeling variations are demonstrated in the *Burn Your Chair* bonus resource guide at *www.burnyourchair. com.*

Kneeling is a challenging posture for many people. Using bolsters and blankets to modify the shape is a good way to make it more available.

A Caution for the Practice of Kneeling

When starting this book, I knew that people in pain-free societies utilize kneeling as a common resting posture. I also noticed it was a shape that children move into instinctively. Combined with the improvements I noticed in my body from the posture, I felt confident in labeling kneeling an essential healing posture.

When seeking scientific evidence to support this idea, I found conflicting reports. Some studies demonstrate that kneeling for long periods of time could pose potential risks by reducing blood flow to the legs. Most of the studies were done in Japan, where sitting seiza is a traditional posture assumed when performing rituals like the Japanese tea ceremony. People in Japan who suffer knee injuries want to be able to attain the kneeling shape again, as it is an important part of their culture. The studies were designed to determine whether or not it was safe to reintroduce kneeling as part of a recovery plan. Some studies found that prolonged kneeling decreases tissue oxygenation in the legs due to compression of the legs, the same compression that helps improve hip, knee, and ankle flexibility and reduces leg swelling. Since chronically deoxygenated tissues cause us pain, these studies made me stop and think about whether or not to include kneeling as an essential healing posture.

This evidence conflicted with what I had been learning about pain-free societies in other studies. In "Sitting, squatting, and the evolutionary biology of human inactivity," scientists report their findings following the Hadza, hunter-gatherers native to Tanzania who do not share our propensity for chronic pain and biomarkers for cardiovascular disease. It's not at all surprising that the Hadza engage in significantly more physical activity than we do. What is surprising is that they spend nine to ten hours a day sedentary, about the same as Western societies.[2]

Just like Dr. Francine Barone noted (see Chapter 2), the scientists from the Hadza study point out that the difference between us and pain-free people is not that we are less active or more sedentary; it's how we choose to hold ourselves while sedentary. The Hadza spend about 12.5 percent of their time in kneeling postures and 18 percent squatting. This suggests that kneeling and squatting are essential shapes for aiding the logistics of human life that is unassisted by techno environments. But does that mean they should be labeled essential for self-healing?

When the scientists from the Hadza study tested the effects of these shapes on the body, they discovered "ground-sitting"

Many cultures utilize kneeling as a part of their traditions. It is seen as a symbol of respect and attentiveness.

postures elicit significantly higher muscle activation than chair sitting. They posit that the gentle muscular demands imposed by entering, exiting, and maintaining postures like squatting and kneeling are enough to create significant health benefits as opposed to the lack of demands and deactivating effects of chair sitting. They even refer to this practice as "active rest" as I do. High levels of unused sugar, cholesterol, and fat circulating in our blood at rest set us up for metabolic and cardiovascular diseases. The light muscular activity generated through active rest encourages the body to utilize free energy, preventing excess energy storage (weight gain) and plaque buildup in the blood vessels.

In Japan, seiza is a symbol of attentiveness, courtesy, and submission to authority. It is the preferred posture for meditation in many other traditional cultures. This is why the seiza studies measured the effects of very long periods of kneeling—around 30 minutes! This does not mimic the short bouts of kneeling interspersed with movement performed throughout the day like a child or hunter-gatherer would do. With a little research of anecdotal evidence, I discovered it is actually common knowledge in Japan that prolonged periods of time spent in seiza lead to "numbness of the legs." This explains why seiza was not a posture commonly held by the warrior class of ancient Japan, since they could not spring into action as quickly after kneeling for too long.

When I first began the practice of kneeling, my body asked me to cycle out of the position quickly, often in less than a minute. After practicing consistently for a few months, I felt encouraged to stay longer, as I found release within the discomfort. Yet I have never felt encouraged to stay for 30 minutes! The signals to shift shape are too loud. It goes without saying that holding any shape for too long will cause problems. The deoxygenation effect found in long periods of kneeling is just another piece of evidence supporting the importance of posture cycling. Cycling through active rest shapes like kneeling increases our baseline muscle activity and metabolism, keeping us pain-free and less likely to die from lifestyle-based diseases. Without the ability to kneel, we lose many functional movement capabilities. Therefore I feel confident in labeling kneeling an essential healing posture.

As with all the postures and practices I offer in this book, I present a simple caution when practicing kneeling. Remember, too much of anything is never healthy. Whether we're talking about kneeling, exercising, or eating kale, the success of all practices requires mindfulness of moderation. Your body contains not only the ability to self-heal but also the ability to self-diagnose. If something stops feeling safe, stop doing it.

Practice—Kneeling

1. Find a soft and relatively flat surface to practice on. Come to a quadruped position, all fours. Add padding below the kneecaps to your comfort level.
2. With hands still on the ground, push your hips back towards your heels. If they touch without intense discomfort, take weight out of the hands by sitting back towards the heels. Add support between the calves and thighs or below your seat as needed.

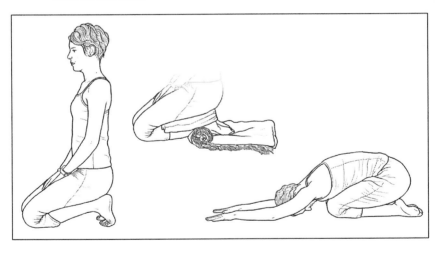

Like sitting on the ground, the kneeling posture has many useful variations, each of which modifies the effect of the pose. Tucking the toes in "toe squat" stretches the plantar fascia and raises the seat slightly. "Child's pose" (kneeling with the head on the ground and arms outstretched) takes pressure off the knees and lengthens the upper body. If kneeling is too uncomfortable to sustain in the ankles, a rolled-up blanket is an excellent support.

3. If it feels safe, sit all the way back, placing your hips on your heels and erecting your spine over your hips. With each breath in, send your head straight up and tip your hips forward. Exhaling, align your spine over your heels by slightly leaning back.

8

Squatting
(Malasana/Shagamu)

"There is simply no other exercise, and certainly no machine, that produces the level of central nervous system activity, improved balance and coordination, skeletal loading and bone density enhancement, muscular stimulation and growth, connective tissue stress and strength, psychological demand and toughness, and overall systemic conditioning than the correctly performed full squat."

—Mark Rippetoe

Benefits: *Improves Hip/Knee/Ankle Mobility, Strengthens and Stabilizes the Lower Body and Core Muscles, Aids in Digestion and Elimination, Decompresses the Low Back, Aids Prenatal Preparation and Delivery in Childbirth, Improves Balance, Improves Functionality of and Links Movement Patterns*

Counter Position: *Standing/Walking, Inversion*

Daily Goal: *Five Minutes or More*

Of all the positions lost from the physical vernacular of modern man, the squat position is arguably the most vital to our health. Once lost, it can feel almost impossible to regain. In the age of bouncing back and forth from sedentary living to short and intense bouts of exercise, physical educators refer to the squat as the most important movement for developing strength and mobility in the largest muscle systems and joints in our bodies. The ability to squat allows us to perform and link various other movements, thus improving the functionality of our bodies.

For toddlers, squat is the primary loading and landing position for many failed attempts at walking. Before taking their first steps, children can already perform many variations of the previously mentioned postures: sitting, kneeling, and sphinx. But until they discover the squat, their ability to hold an unassisted vertical position will be weak at best. Toddlers instinctively utilize the squat as a stable base to lift themselves up from, as the structure of this shape creates an excellent framework to leverage the power of the lower body.

As demonstrated by every child as they learn to walk, the squat is a vital part of developing and maintaining the strength and suppleness of the human body.

While pursuing my degree in physical education, many professors showed us pictures of toddlers in the squat position as a reference for teaching adults proper form. It wasn't until I watched my daughter's development from infant to toddler that I realized the significance of this shape beyond weightlifting. I saw Joy perform dozens of squats throughout the day, assisted by grabbing onto whatever was around her. This exercise program helped her build up the strength needed for standing and walking unassisted. The action of rising up and squatting down many times throughout the day and ideally over the course of one's lifetime is one of the most important physical actions for maintaining the strength and suppleness of the body. Joy squats instinctively when going to the bathroom, inspecting a leaf, or playing with her toys, just as adults living in pain-free societies do.

To a child, the squat is a link to other postures and movement patterns that make the world more available. After sitting on the ground for a while, Joy will kneel, then push herself into a forward

8. Squatting (Malasana/Shagamu)

folding position and finally to a squat in order to rise up and walk away. You can imagine my pride, thinking that I have passed on some kind of special yoga gene. Really, she's just following basic human instincts to make her movements more ergonomic, aiding her exploration and making more independence possible. If encouraged, these instincts extend into adulthood, as they do with the billions of people around the world who still rest, poop, and give birth in squat every day.

According to a recent poll of 2,500 Westerners, we spend an average of an hour and 45 minutes per week sitting on the toilet, twice as long as we spend exercising.[1] That's 92 days over the course of our lifetime, or 15 minutes a day slumped over a porcelain bowl, longer if we get stuck in a phone hole scrolling through fake news. In pain-free societies, that time is spent in the squat position, requiring muscular and mental engagement, balance and coordination. Humans have squatted to relieve themselves for thousands of years. The invention of the toilet removed the need for this simple and therapeutic movement pattern. Instead of holding ourselves upright with alert posture in a complex functional position, we sit disengaged in one more chair.

Evidence suggests that squatting to go number two takes half as long as sitting on the toilet and reduces straining.[2] Squatting makes going to the bathroom easier because it allows the puborectalis muscle to relax more easily, widening the pathway for stool to escape. In squat the legs are folded up against the abdomen, putting pressure on the gut to further aid motility. Going to the bathroom in a squat has been shown to alleviate chronic symptoms like painful bowel movements, anal fissures, passing blood, and trouble sitting from the aforementioned issues.[3] Additionally, bathrooms designed for squatting instead of sitting are more hygienic, as no part of the body needs to touch any surfaces when squatting to go to the bathroom.

Okay, that's enough potty talk. Let's further examine the physical demands of the deep squat. Holding a deep squatting posture requires full flexion of the knees, hips and ankles. For most people this means a fairly intense stretch of the inner thighs and low back as well as compression in the knees. To maintain this position, we must intelligently engage muscles in our feet, legs, and core in ways that are unique to the demands of standing and sitting. We must unite this muscular engagement with the brain centers that cultivate balance. Holding onto this engagement at end range improves the mobility of our joints. Greater mobility improves functionality by allowing us to be more agile and to generate more power.

In terms of pain relief, the squat addresses the largest joints and muscles in the body while also affecting one of the most common sites of chronic pain, the low back. When we hold a deep squat, our tail naturally tucks under, relieving the hips from the anterior pelvic tilt that supports health sitting and standing posture. This pulls into a stretch the muscles of the low back and the interconnected hip muscles and fascia. All of this tissue relief lends itself to the most important ancient

Leaning back against something can make squatting more doable. If the squat is a challenging shape for you, turn your back to a wall, leaving one foot's distance between your heels and the wall. With your feet hip distance apart and toes pointing slightly outward, hinge at the waist to touch the ground. Keeping your hands on the ground, lean your hips against the wall. Slowly bend at the knees, keeping your weight against the wall until you reach an edge you can maintain for a bit. If the squat is easier for you, simply lean against the wall from standing, and slide down into "wall squat."

practice of all: childbirth. Mothers around the world are rejecting the cold and traumatic ways birth and prenatal care are handled by allopathic medicine. Squatting as a prenatal practice lengthens and relaxes the tissues of the lower body, the internal sphincters, and the perineum. This results in easier, less painful, and less complicated births. During labor, many women report variations of squatting

8. Squatting (Malasana/Shagamu)

and kneeling alleviate some of their pain. Furthermore, upright birthing positions have been shown to generate stronger feelings of birth satisfaction than the one posture made available in hospitals: reclining.[4]

Studies comparing the effects of squatting versus the typical reclined posture of a hospital bed demonstrate evidence that the squat may even make labor shorter. Additionally, mothers who squat to deliver have been shown to require sig-

Squatting as a prenatal practice can prepare the body for a less-complicated birth. Upright birthing positions such as squatting and kneeling have been shown to shorten labor time and improve a mother's birth experience.

nificantly less labor stimulation from pharmaceuticals, which means fewer side effects and complications. Squat births are much less likely to result in perineal tears, reduces their severity when they do occur, and results in less episiotomies (a surgical cut made at the opening of the vagina during childbirth to aid a difficult delivery and prevent rupture of tissues). Squat births are also significantly less likely to require mechanical interventions such as the use of forceps to deliver the baby.[5]

Given all the mechanical and logistical advantages of the squatting position, combined with the fact that it provides both therapeutic and performance-enhancing benefits, it is arguably one of the most important positions available in the human body. However, many people will find squat to be the most challenging of the eight essential healing postures. If this is the case for you, it is important to seek out the modifications for squatting that suit your body best. Look at the illustrations in this chapter for inspiring your search for squatting shapes that work for you.

Practice—Squat

1. Stand with your heels below your hips, and turn your toes slightly outward. Reach your hands towards the ground as you hinge at the hips, allowing your knees to naturally bend, and sit your hips down towards your heels. If it feels impossible to enter squat this way, grab onto something to support yourself on the way down, or lean back against a wall and slowly slide down.

2. If you're having trouble balancing, keep your hands on something supportive or place them on the ground if possible. If you desire a more active shape, remove your hands from support. Bring your elbows to your inner thighs, and press your palms together in prayer, creating a frame that pushes the legs open with each exhale.

3. Whether you are keeping your hands on the floor, placing them in prayer, or taking another modification, it is important not to lift your heels off the ground unless you are very mobile and experienced in the squatting position. With each inhale attempt to lengthen your spine, sending your head straight up. With each exhale, lean your weight back

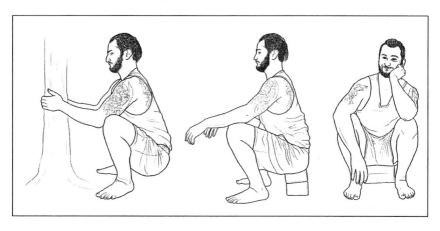

Be creative in supporting yourself in squat. Grab onto something in front of you if you feel like you are going to fall back. Boost your hips with a stack of books or a short stool. Sit on a staircase with your hips on a higher stair and your legs arranged in a squatting shape on a lower stair.

8. Squatting (Malasana/Shagamu)

slightly into your heels and try to relax the parts of you that are experiencing edges.

4. It's important when squatting to carefully consider how you will exit. Usually the best exit is determined by how long you have held the shape. If you are injury-free and relatively strong, standing up out of a squat you've held for a short time after properly bracing your muscles and adjusting your posture is a great exit. However, it is inadvisable to push straight up out of a squatting position you have held for longer than a minute (or longer than you're used to) unless again you are very experienced in moving your body in this way. Gentler exits are to either lean back to sit on the ground, to lean forward to kneel, or come into a standing forward fold before rising back up.

To modify the squat, place your hands on a railing or piece of furniture. Lean against a wall or place something underneath the seat. Sit on a stoop or staircase, and arrange the legs in the squatting shape on a stair below. More squat modifications are provided in the *Burn Your Chair* bonus resource guide at *www.burnyourchair.com*. Whichever modification you take, focus on lengthening your spine as you breathe. Inhaling, reach the crown higher; exhaling, attempt an anterior pelvic tilt. As this is one of the most intense of the eight essential postures, it requires the most caution and patience. Find the variations that work best for you, and remember to rest in counterposes when the body signals you to do so.

9

Standing/Walking
(Sthiti/Tatsu)

*"It's your road and yours alone. Others may walk it
with you, but no one can walk it for you."*—Rumi

Benefits: *Improves Posture, Cardiovascular Health, Pulmonary
Health, Metabolic Health, Reduces Blood Sugar and Insulin Resis-
tance, Helps Control Weight, Eases Joint Pain and Muscle Stiffness,
Increases Muscle Strength and Endurance, Strengthens Bones,
Improves Balance, Improves Mood and Mental Health, Boosts
Energy, Aids in Managing Conditions such as Diabetes/High Blood
Pressure/High Cholesterol, Boosts Immunity, Extends Lifespan,
Improves Public Health and Protects the Environment*

Counter Position: *Hanging*

Daily Goal: *Two Hours or More*

About 6,000,000 years ago, our ancestors began evolving to
travel upright. This came from a need to carry our food and children across long distances to explore grasslands. It allowed us to
reach low-hanging fruit without climbing and made us appear
larger and more intimidating. Standing upright was the last piece
of the evolutionary puzzle that put humans at the top of the food
chain.

But being upright comes at a cost. Supporting all of our weight
on two limbs is tiring, and in this position gravity compresses our
spine all day. Some pain specialists theorize that back pain and other
skeletal issues are due to the change from quadrupedal to bipedal.
Reverting to all fours is obviously not the answer to our pain, but
standing and walking are no longer necessary for survival due to

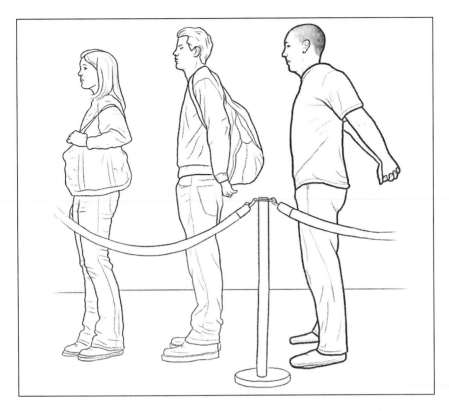

Standing is the ideal position for most forms of work. Compared to sitting in a chair, standing opens up a world of posture and movement possibilities. Walking is the most useful and effective form of exercise available in the human body. These two practices alone could end much of the suffering caused by modern lifestyle.

advances in technology. So instead of bearing the burden of standing and walking, we work and rest in chairs and travel in cars.

In order to achieve maximum wellness, we must combine regular doses of standing and walking with the decompression found in active rest postures. Without sufficient amounts of both, our bodies are guaranteed to develop painful dysfunction, and our risk of premature death grows. In regards to modernized cultures, human evolution has paused. If our evolution is to resume, we need more than mere survival. We need to thrive.

With a better balance of sitting and standing at work, productivity improves and sick days are fewer. Healthcare costs are lower, and employee morale is higher. Standing desks, variable desks, and even treadmill desks are making office environments more like natural environments by allowing workers to vary the pressures placed on their bodies throughout the workday. Combining working upright with taking short walks throughout the workday results in workers being happier and healthier, making their companies more successful.

As you can see from the long list at the beginning of the chapter, the benefits of standing and walking are so numerous that it's easy to label them essential for healing. Some of the benefits of standing and walking are the same, with many of these benefits increasing significantly in effect when walking. Let's focus first on the effects of periodically standing up to work versus only working from a chair. As you will see, the evidence supporting the practice is extensive.

Take a Stand

A recent study conducted by the Mayo Clinic reveals that standing for six hours per day instead of sitting in a chair significantly lowers the risk of obesity.[1] Standing for six hours is a lot, especially if you're just getting started. Thankfully, evidence also indicates that small doses of standing accumulate into significant health benefits. By measuring oxygen consumption as a reflection of calories burned, scientists have determined that on average we burn 80 calories per hour when seated and 88 calories per hour when standing. This means standing at your desk for three hours a day instead of sitting burns an extra 24 calories, about the same as a carrot. Not exactly a huge difference. However, walking burns an average of 210 calories per hour, about the same as in a Snickers bar.[2]

One could argue that the slightly higher calorie burn from standing instead of sitting in a chair could add up over time. But the cardiometabolic advantages to standing regularly throughout the day add up to more than a few carrots or the occasional candy bar. Researchers in Australia found that standing increases your "good" HDL cholesterol and decreases your "bad" LDL cholesterol. Trading standing for sitting for an extra two hours per day was shown to improve HDL cholesterol by 0.06 mmol/L and lower LDL cholesterol by 6 percent. Furthermore, standing was associated with a 2 percent lower fasting blood sugar level and an 11 percent lower level of triglycerides on average. In fact, this study demonstrated that every two hours spent sitting each day was associated with increased weight, waist size, blood sugar, and bad cholesterol, thereby increasing the risk of cardiovascular and metabolic diseases.[3]

Another study from the American Diabetes Association showed that breaking up long periods of sitting with standing or light walking dropped blood sugar levels by as much as 34 percent in overweight women who had poor glucose regulation, a risk factor for diabetes. Choosing to stand more often instead of sitting in chairs can help prevent type 2 diabetes by lowering blood sugar and insulin resistance. This practice can also help people who already have type 2 diabetes to manage their condition.[4]

In 2018 the American Cancer Society declared that prolonged sitting, even in those who exercise regularly, increases the risk of developing cancer. However, even as little as a one-minute break

Standing is a great counter position for sitting. It makes a wide array of stretches and exercises available to help us shake off stagnation and revitalize our bodies. By reaching, bending, and folding from a standing position, we can utilize leverage and gravity to aid in releasing tension.

from sitting can reduce molecules in the body that are linked with cancer risk.[5] Several synonymous studies suggest that prolonged periods of sitting in chairs lead to a shorter lifespan.

A meta-analysis of 16 studies and 800,000 participants found that those with the greatest amount of time spent sitting had 112 percent greater risk of developing diabetes, 147 percent greater risk of cardiovascular events, 90 percent higher chance of dying from those events, and a 49 percent increased risk of all-cause mortality.[6] A similar study suggested that replacing sitting with standing for three hours per day could net us an extra two years of life expectancy.[7]

The benefits of standing more go beyond extended lifespan. Most of us would agree that living longer is ideal, but there's also much to be said about the quality of the life we're living. If you suffer from chronic pain, the quality of your life is severely diminished. A study conducted at Stanford University examined the effect of sit-stand workstations on back pain in 46 office workers. Participants with adjustable workstations were significantly more likely to report a pain-free day than the control group who sat. They also reported a significant reduction in both their current back pain and the worst incidences of back pain over the three-month period.[8]

Evidence from a similar study suggests that standing up to work improves mood and increases perceived energy level. In 2011 the "Take-A-Stand Project" followed sedentary workers who were given sit-stand devices for their workstations for seven weeks. Given the ability to stand and the education of what it might do for them, participants decreased their sitting time by 224 percent. This large reduction in sitting time correlated with a 54 percent reduction in reported pain symptoms, increased energy levels and improved mood. Furthermore, the removal of the sit-stand device during the post-intervention period largely negated the observed improvements within just two weeks.[9]

Another study published in *Occupational and Environmental Medicine* reports that transitioning between a seated and standing position every 30 minutes during the workday can significantly reduce fatigue and low back discomfort. For this study, participants performed typical tasks for eight hours each day either sitting in a chair or alternating between standing and sitting every 30 minutes.

Participants reported significantly more low back pain when they sat for the entire eight hours compared to the group who was alternating between sitting and standing. Their total fatigue scores also dropped, and their overall productivity increased.[10]

Indeed, evidence demonstrates that standing up to work reduces the incidence of pain, boosts energy levels and improves mood. However, it's the increase in productivity found standing that is grabbing the attention of major corporations. A 2014 article in *Social, Psychological, and Personality Science* found that teams of workers in stand-up workspaces had higher arousal levels, lower levels of conflict, and more collaborative creativity when problem-solving together.[11] More companies need to be made aware of the profitability of making this change in order for a cultural shift this drastic to be successful.

A similar study found that call center agents who used a stand-capable desk over the course of six months were more productive than their coworkers who used regular desks. Workers at the stand-capable desks were on average 45 percent more productive than their seated colleagues. Additionally, the productivity of the stand-capable desk users significantly increased over time, from about 23 percent in the first month to about 53 percent over the next six months, demonstrating that the benefits of standing up to work increase with practice.[12] This is because standing, much like the other seven essential healing postures, offers freedom of movement not found when glued to a chair.

The benefits of standing up more throughout our day are numerous. Just like the other practices offered in this book, a standing practice is something that should be started carefully and maintained with mindfulness. Some studies are beginning to reveal evidence that too much standing too soon can cause pain in people who are very accustomed to sitting. I believe this is because people are standing still for too long with poor standing posture, which causes the same problems we find bound to chairs. When starting a standing practice, start small and listen to the edges that are present in your body. Visit the *Burn Your Chair* bonus resource guide at *www.burnyourchair.com* to learn more about standing up at work as well as various postures and stretches that are available in the standing position.

Practice—Active Standing

1. To stand actively, place your heels below your hips and allow your feet to turn slightly outward. Let your shoulders roll back, and draw your head back over your neck, slightly tucking your chin.

2. Lift up all of your toes and spread them out; then press them down into the ground. Press the toes down so firmly that you feel the arches of your feet slightly lift.

3. Brace your lower body by squeezing together your glutes and thighs. It's as if you are "screwing your legs into the ground," but your legs don't actually rotate because your feet are firmly planted.

4. Finally, engage your core to unite the lower body and torso. Find even, mindful breathing within this shape.

5. On an exhale, relax half of the muscle tension you have generated to stand actively, while attempting to maintain your posture. This will make the position manageable for longer periods of time.

Oftentimes the reason we find standing for long periods painful is because we stand with disengaged posture. Just like when we sit slumped in a chair, standing disengaged compresses the body and induces lethargy. By standing actively, we support the hips and back with muscular engagement. This may feel a bit more tiring, but it has the simultaneous advantages of strengthening the body, encouraging fullness of breath, and preventing pain.

Many military traditions encourage this type of standing so that troops can maintain their attention and physical preparedness for long periods of time. The active standing position has also been observed in indigenous populations. It protects the low back from taking all of our weight, strengthens our core, and encourages the full depth of our breath. Standing actively with the glutes and core engaged is a bit of a workout. In fact, clients have told me that their glutes were sore after their first time practicing active standing at work. Try to develop a gentler baseline of contraction over time by practicing regularly so that when you stand for long periods of time it is manageable.

Standing actively throughout the day prevents postural problems that lead to pain. However, it is a challenging practice to maintain, especially if you spend long periods of time working in the standing position. Sometimes your mind will be focusing more on the task at hand than the needs of the body. Soon this will lead to poor posture and tension, which left unchecked will cause pain. An excellent biofeedback exercise for reawakening healthy standing posture is the pelvic tilt exercise from Chapter 1. Perform a few standing pelvic tilts anytime you notice your low back fatiguing. This will reawaken the glutes and create a blood pump that directs heat and hydration to the low back.

If you continue to experience pain, your body is telling you to either walk it off, rest, change positions, or change how and where you stand. Standing on anti-fatigue padding such as a folded-up yoga mat may make standing longer more doable. However, it's important to remember that standing is just another posture to cycle into and out of. There are endless variations to explore while standing that may make it so you can stand longer, but the other seven essential healing postures are always there for you when your body says it's time for change.

Walking the Path of Self-Healing

The benefits of being upright increase exponentially when we walk, especially if we choose to walk in natural environments. Walking is the most commonly prescribed form of exercise because it is the most accessible mode available and holds the best risk-to-reward ratio. After open-heart surgery, how far the patient can walk is an indicator of how ready they are to return home. Walking is an ancient pastime that brings together neighbors and communities. Combined with mindfulness the practice of walking becomes a powerful meditation. The joy of walking gives us access to some of the most amazing places on Earth that are only accessible by foot.

When we walk, we burn more than double the calories burned per hour while standing still (moving at a moderate pace, around three mph). Actual caloric burn will vary based on factors such as total distance covered, terrain, speed, and your body composition. This increase in energy expenditure lowers blood sugar and circulating triglycerides, helping to prevent or manage conditions such as diabetes and heart disease.

A study published in *Diabetes Care* showed that walking significantly improved daily glycemic control in older adults, whether they chose one longer bout of walking (around 45 minutes) or three shorter bouts (15 minutes each) spaced out throughout the day. If the three shorter bouts occurred right after meals, blood sugar

The benefits of walking are numerous. Walking protects our physical, mental, and spiritual health. It is the safest and most accessible form of exercise we can partake in. After a period of stagnation, going for a walk activates our body, improves our mood, and clears our mind.

control was even more impressive.[13] A similar study published in the *European Journal of Epidemiology* found that walking at a comfortable pace for 30 minutes a day, five days a week, led to a 19 percent decreased risk of coronary heart disease.[14]

Walking has also been shown to be an effective treatment for chronic pain. A recent study published in the *American Journal of Preventive Medicine* followed 1,564 adults over age 49 who had joint pain stemming from osteoarthritis. Researchers asked participants to walk each week as a preventative measure to keep their pain from reaching disability status. Results found that as little as one hour per week of moderate-to-vigorous pace walking was enough to prevent disability due to joint pain for the four years of the study as well as increase mobility and independence.[15]

One could go on and on about the evidence supporting the benefits of walking regularly. It is fair to say instead that the aforementioned benefits of standing simply become more dramatic when walking is added to the practice. What really sets walking apart from standing and other healing practices are the benefits it provides to the psyche and the spirit. Recall the teachings of Dr. Sarno outlined in Chapter 4. It is arguably more important to strengthen our mental and spiritual bodies than it is to strengthen our physical body when it comes to defeating chronic pain.

Research has demonstrated repeatedly that walking improves our mood, sparks creativity, and can alleviate symptoms like depression, anxiety, and mental illness. What's even more interesting is that new research indicates that if we walk outside, particularly in green spaces, near water or in other sensually captivating environments, the effects are exponentially increased. A study published in *Applied Psychology* measured affect in young adults before and after 40 minutes of walking. Some of the walks were performed streetside and others in parks, some with friends and some alone. For all the participants positive affect increased and negative affect decreased after walking. Walks in the park decreased feelings of time pressure and increased feelings of revitalization, and walking with friends increased positive feelings regardless of location.[16]

These findings are important because they give us evidence that we have natural antidepressants available to us at any time just by walking out the door. A similar study followed 137 visitors to a national heritage site in the UK to measure the effects of a long walk on their mood and self-esteem. Most participants arrived by car, so they had been sitting for some time. Before and after their tour of the site, they were interviewed to determine their feelings of self-esteem and their current mood states. Participants reported a significant increase in self-esteem after the walk. Furthermore, visitors leaving the green sites were significantly less angry, tense, depressed and confused compared to when they were just arriving. They felt significantly more energetic, and longer stays were associated with greater increases in overall mood.[17]

Reading this study I wondered if similar increases in mood and self-esteem would be reported by those who have mental health problems, since anxiety, depression, and substance abuse are often linked to long-term pain. A study published in *Health and Place* examined the differences between people with good mental health and those with poor mental health after a walking intervention. Walks were performed in both urban and rural environments by both groups. Results supported previously cited findings that walks in rural environments create more restorative benefits than urban walks. Those with poorer mental health received significantly greater benefits regardless of the setting.[18]

We need to encourage each other to walk more often. The practice of walking holds the power to strengthen family ties, to unite neighbors and communities. It can be a form of prayer or a form of protest. Walking together seems to physically and energetically connect us, much like singing together in choir. Improving the mental and physical health of individual community members means a healthier community at large. A meta-analysis of literature on the physical, mental, and communal benefits of walking published by the American College of Sports Medicine declares:

> *"Indeed, if everyone in the United States began walking 30–60 min each day, the benefits would be extensive. Although it is currently difficult to quantify all the effects, one predicts lower rates of chronic diseases (such as obesity and CVD) and a dramatic reduction in medical expenditures, with only a modest increase in number of activity-related injuries. Because walking is the most popular type of moderate intensity physical activity, walking has substantial importance to public health. We reach the interesting conclusion that part of the solution to chronic disease and rising health care costs is as simple as walking everyday."[19]*

9. Standing/Walking (Sthiti/Tatsu)

Since it is so accessible and the effects are doubled when in the company of others, walking has a unifying power. At a time when Western cultures are so heavily divided and violently polarized, this benefit is invaluable. People have been marching together to stand up for what they believe in since time immemorial. The simple act of walking together has sparked revolutions and encouraged evolution of the human family.

Practice—Mindful Walking

1. Find a change of scenery, preferably somewhere peaceful and natural. Remove your shoes if possible.
2. Walk slowly enough so that you can deeply tune into your sense of touch. Feel the ground beneath your feet. Experience texture changes from one surface to another. Use the information you receive from your feet to help you modify your pace and the pressure placed in each step.
3. Attune to your other senses. Broaden your vision to take in as much as possible rather than only looking down at your feet. Periodically focus on this or that. Listen closely to the sounds around you. Smell the air. Feel the temperature of the environment in contrast to that of your body.
4. Experiment with combining this practice with mindful breathing. Count how many steps you take with each inhale and exhale. Play with making the exhales longer to encourage relaxation or lengthen the inhales to energize. For a deeply serene yet somewhat challenging practice, try taking one step per inhale and one step per exhale.

10

Hanging
(Lambita/Burasagaru)

"Success seems to be largely a matter of hanging on when others have let go."—William Feather

Benefits: *Decompresses the Spine/Shoulders/Arms, Improves Grip and Upper Body Strength, Improves Shoulder Mobility and Overall Shoulder Health, Reshapes the Rotator Cuff, Aids in Shoulder Injury Repair, Corrects Posture, Prevents Disability*
Counter Position: *Standing and Walking*
Daily Goal: *One Minute or More*

Millions of people suffer daily from painful conditions and disabilities stemming from lack of upper body strength and mobility. About 26 percent of the population is affected by shoulder pain from shoulder impingement, rotator cuff injuries, and "frozen shoulder syndrome."[1] The most commonly prescribed treatments for these conditions are rest, physical therapy, and pain medication. If the problem persists, surgeries are prescribed. But research from the University of Helsinki demonstrates that the most common shoulder surgeries used for treating shoulder pain are no more effective than placebo surgeries.[2] Luckily, there is an ancient human practice that has the power to heal and prevent shoulder pain.

Long before our ancestors stood upright to venture out across the savannah, the jungle canopy was their preferred habitat. Climbing and hanging from trees, they reached for fresh fruits, found protection from predators, and shelter from the elements. The requirements of daily life kept their grip strong and our shoulders supple. Although modern man still maintains these abilities, they no longer mean the difference between life and death. Yet left unused, complex body systems like our shoulders atrophy, become dysfunctional, and cause us pain. We existed as hunter-gatherers for 99.6 percent of our history. Our time as farmers and urbanites only represents 0.4 percent of human existence.[3] This 0.4 percent slice of life is the time in which we evolved into our propensity towards chronic pain. To reverse this phenomenon, we need to exercise regularly the capabilities of our bodies that are no longer required for survival.

Dr. John Kirsch is an orthopedic surgeon who literally wrote the book on healing shoulder pain.[4] He had suffered a shoulder injury himself, and much like Dr. Sarno (mentioned in Chapter 4) Kirsch noticed that surgeries

Hanging was a crucial ability for our ancestors. It opened up many options for gathering food, traveling, finding shelter, and hiding from predators. Although it is no longer necessary for our survival, this lost practice still holds many benefits for modern bodies.

didn't seem to provide long-term results, so he looked for other ways to treat his pain. He had a hunch that hanging from a bar might help, so he started to hang for a couple of minutes a day. In a few months, his shoulder pain was gone. He subsequently designed an exercise protocol that utilized hanging as the main intervention and began offering it to his patients with shoulder pain.

The success of his protocol was so great that Dr. Kirsh performed his own study to quantify the effects. Of the 92 participants who suffered from shoulder impingement, rotator cuff tears, adhesive capsulitis (frozen shoulder), or osteoarthritis of the glenohumeral joint diagnosed by MRI scan, 90 returned to comfortably performing activities of daily living, while the two who did not complete the

Exploring variations of hanging is a great way to receive the same benefits without entering the full posture. Hanging variations are available all around us: on the subway, in the park, and above every door we walk through.

exercise program did not. Moreover, many of the subjects who were initially prescribed surgery were able to forgo their operation after performing Kirsh's protocol.

Kirsch began researching the structure of the shoulder to figure out why hanging from a bar can help heal shoulder injuries. Using CT scan X-ray technology, Kirsh filmed the position of shoulder tissues in various movements and positions, including the hanging posture. Kirsh theorizes that when we go years without using the full range of motion of our shoulders, the acromion (a bony protrusion of our shoulder blade that meets our clavicle) begins to curve. This shrinks the gap (called the subacromial space) between the acromion and the humerus (the upper arm bone). Various tendons and tissues vital to shoulder health live in that gap, and when the gap shrinks, the likelihood of bones rubbing and pinching these tendons increases. The rubbing and pinching of these tendons causes shoulder impingement, the most common type of shoulder injury. According to Kirsh's research, regularly hanging can help straighten out a curved acromion, which increases the gap in the subacromial space, reducing pinching and friction and allowing the shoulder to heal.

The benefits of hanging go beyond simply reducing friction within the shoulder joint. After long periods of standing, walking, or sitting, your body may start asking for relief from the compressive force of gravity. Recall the image offered for sphinx pose; think of your body like a spring. The natural space between each vertebra and joint is like the space between the spring's coils. While upright, the weight of our body compresses our joints and the tissues in-between them (such as the vertebral discs), making the spring tighter and creating potential energy.

If we remain compressed like this too long without seeking relief or expelling our potential energy, the joints are never given the breathing room they need to rest and repair. Hanging creates a chain of traction from our hands to our hips, decompressing all of the joints along the way, most notably our shoulders and spine. It's as if we were able to pull apart the spring that is our spine. By decompressing the spine through positions like sphinx and hanging, joint tissues naturally achieve greater length. This creates the space necessary for hydration to flow in and relubricate joint surfaces.

Get a Grip

While I was awaiting the birth of my daughter, I liked to ask parents what their favorite memories of their child coming into the world were. Many recounted for me the first time their infant child grabbed hold of them with a strong grip. It was a sign that their child was healthy, that they were going to thrive. After hearing these stories, I anxiously anticipated the first time my child would grab hold of me. Within a few hours of being born, Joy's innate strength proved true as she wrapped her whole hand around my little finger and squeezed with surprising force.

This infantile ability to make a strong grip is known as the palmar grasp reflex and is indicative of our ancient need to cling to our parents as they swung from tree to tree or traveled the savannah in search of food. Many modern children maintain and further develop a strong grip throughout their upbringing. Their instinct to play has them hanging or swinging from anything overhead. As adults, most of us will replace our instincts for health-promoting play with the habits of modern life. We lose the benefits that arise from following the innate wisdom of our body. Research indicates that poor grip strength is a strong predictor of adult disability and premature death.[5]

The more you hang, the more strength you will build in your hands and by proxy the tendons and muscles of the shoulders and arms. As your hand and upper body strength increases, you will be capable of hanging longer and able to support more of your own weight without assistance. Additionally, as your grip strength improves, you will feel more comfortable relaxing your other muscles, allowing for more shoulder and spinal traction. Like all active rest practices, the benefits of hanging are cumulative. The more you hang, the better you'll feel; and if the evidence cited in the previous paragraph proves true, the more you hang, the longer you'll live.

Practice—
Passive Hang

1. Find an overhead bar, tree branch, or something else from your environment that you can grip with your whole hand, that is sturdy

We envy the strong, healthy, and resilient bodies of children, gymnasts, and other climbers. The hanging posture and the movements it makes possible allow us to receive many of the same physical qualities without the backflips and somersaults.

enough to support more than your body weight and that is just slightly shorter than the length of your outstretched arms when standing.

2. Grip the bar firmly, wrapping all the fingers around, ensuring that the thumb encircles the bar and the pinky wraps as far around it as possible.

3. Slowly bend your legs until you're supporting an amount of weight that you feel capable of holding for a little while.

4. Focus on your breathing, paying special attention to the exhales. Each exhale try to disengage all of the muscles of your body other than those in your hands and forearms. Encourage especially the shoulder, core, and hip muscles to be slack to receive the most traction possible.

With consistent practice you will eventually become strong enough to hold all of your weight off of the

Our complex shoulder joint was an evolutionary adaptation that ensured our survival millions of years ago. Now that we no longer hang and perform other movements that exercise the shoulder as it was designed to be, stagnation and atrophy lead to chronic pain. By simply reintroducing the hanging posture into daily life, we repair the shoulder joint and lengthen the spine, restoring their primal power.

ground. At that time you may find it more comfortable to grip a surface that is just slightly out of standing reach, taking a little hop or using a step of some kind to reach it. This will allow you to be more disengaged in your hips and core, thus allowing full traction.

Make it your goal to accumulate a minute of passive hanging every day. If this becomes easy and you want to continue accruing benefits, start hanging from different surfaces or increase your daily hang time goal. Experiment with pulling exercises and swinging or traveling from a hanging position (brachiating) to take your practice even further. You can find more hanging variations in the *Burn Your Chair* bonus resource guide at *www.burnyourchair.com*.

Once you are comfortable with the hanging posture you can begin experimenting with movements like swinging from bar to bar (braciation). Pulling movements like braciation and climbing develop highly functional upper body strength, enhance coordination, and increase self-confidence.

11

Inversion
(Viparita/Gyakuten)

"It's a good thing to turn your mind upside down now and then, like an hour-glass, to let the particles run the other way."
—Christopher Morley

Benefits: *Improves Heart Rate Variability, Eases Circulation, Stimulates the Lymphatic System, Relieves Fluid Pooling in the Lower Body, Improves Balance, Improves Core Strength, Improves Vagal Tone, Improves Vein Health, Heightens Self-Awareness, Alters Perspective, Increases Confidence, Promotes Relaxation, Improves Gut Health*
Counter Position: *Sitting/Lying on the Ground*
Daily Goal: *Three Minutes or More*

A wise woman once told me that there are three ways children explore their bodies once they realize they have conscious control: They hold their breath, spin, and flip upside down. Her point has been well proven to me, as these activities are three of my daughter's favorite ways to explore sensation.

As an infant, Joy would randomly hold her breath or breathe so slowly it was imperceptible. I was a bit nervous about this behavior and asked our pediatrician about it. She assured me it was completely normal and healthy experimentation that many children display. After that conversation we found ways to encourage Joy to control her breathing more mindfully. She now enjoys sniffing and snuffing rhythmically to energize herself (something she learned from my morning breath practice) and joins us each night in taking three deep breaths before dinner. These practices are tremendously beneficial now that she is a toddler. We can disrupt her tantrums by saying, "I see you're upset. Can you take a deep breath?" With a big sniff and an open-mouth exhale, Joy calms herself down ... most of the time.

Spinning has become her favorite dance move, which she'll do in response to any kind of music, any sound that holds a rhythm, and the songs she sings in her head. There's nothing that makes me happier than seeing my little girl spinning in circles with a huge smile on her face until she falls to the ground laughing. When life is feeling tough and watching isn't enough, joining her in a spinning session helps me shake off the tension too.

Joy went through phases where sleep was elusive. These periods seemed

An inversion posture is any shape where your head is below your heart. Inversions reverse the effect of gravity on the body, easing the flow of fluids back to the organs, heart and brain. Inverting regularly improves our heart rate variability, an indicator of resilience to stress and cardiovascular health.

to coincide with major growth spurts and developmental leaps. These nights were excruciating for everyone, and we tried everything we could think of to help her sleep. One night while rocking my crying child I angled her body downward slightly so her legs were higher than her head. To my amazement, she stopped crying. If I took her out of this position too quickly, she immediately resumed crying. For a few weeks, a gentle inversion was something that seemed to bring her enough of a sensory shift that she could fall sound asleep.

11. Inversion (Viparita/Gyakuten)

Now that she's older, going upside down is something that affects her like spinning. It immediately puts a smile on her face and can totally change her mood. Children enjoy these types of activities because of the sensory input they create. Spinning and inverting have strong effects on the vestibular system, also known as the "inner ear," a sensory system much like that of sight or sound that provides the brain with input about motion and spatial orientation. This lesser-known sixth sense helps us maintain balance, stabilize our body during movement, and maintain posture. Thus, a healthy vestibular system is essential for easeful movement, stability, and equilibrium.

Some children seem to have more of an urge to expose themselves consistently to sensory stimulation than others. A growing body of clinical research is attempting to explain this phenomenon and whether there are advantages to encouraging these behaviors in order to develop the vestibular system early in life. Children who seek out vestibular-stimulating activities (sometimes called "sensory kiddos") may seem distractible, hyper, or unfocused because they can't sit still in school or at the dinner table. When we attempt to control these behaviors, we may be training them out of healthy instincts. Children learn body awareness and control by engaging in this unfocused, high-energy play. The instinct to release physical energy and tension is another example of the body's innate wisdom. Being scolded for these healthy instincts puts children in a tug-of-war between what their body is telling them to do and what adults are asking of them. Non-traditional classrooms like the "invisible classroom" utilized in nature-based education programs encourage children to explore their environment using all of their sensory systems rather than only providing academic information.

It's possible that sensory kiddos might develop to be more physically capable adults who know how to control their bodies and how to effectively expend energy. When their instincts to play are gently encouraged and structured for safety, these children enter into a "gym" or "lab" within their bodies and minds. Unfortunately, this is not generally the case. Their hyperactivity is seen as a nuisance, and teachers are not given the tools or time to adequately address the issue. Some child development specialists suggest that vestibular-stimulating activities such as inverting, swinging, and sliding may calm hyperactivity and return focus.[1] Of course, even children who do not fit the profile of a sensory kiddo benefit from this kind of play.

Children who are sensitive to physical and social stimulation like those on the autism spectrum or highly sensitive persons (HSP) may intentionally avoid vestibular activities to limit sensory input and create a greater sense of safety. Conversely, some children attach to and habitually repeat certain vestibular-stimulating activities to self-soothe.[2] These children process sensory input in a very different way from others, and their responses vary greatly across the spectrum of their disorder. Therefore, it is vitally important to learn about each child's individual reactions to vestibular stimulation in order to create an effective vestibular rehabilitation plan.[3] More research into clinically administered sensory input therapies for children is greatly needed.

Children need encouragement and structure from the adults in their lives to receive a healthy amount of vestibular stimulation. It is a failing of mainstream education to focus on academics and team sports more than play. There is a systemic lack of access to healthy vestibular stimulation for children who need it most. This has created public health problems for our youngest generations. Lack of activity causes children to become restless and "misbehave."

Many children love going upside down. This type of play aids in developing the vestibular system which helps maintain balance, coordination, and posture. When we stop stimulating our vestibular system as adults, it becomes untrained and dysfunctional.

Chronically missing out on these activities affects long-term development, leading to a lifetime of pain and dysfunction.

As we get older and stop playing with the various body positions we are capable of, we lose the multitude of benefits that play offers our bodies. Thankfully, it's easy to regain the physical benefits of play at any age or fitness level. By playing with therapeutic exercise, breath exercise, and holding active rest postures like inversions, we reconnect with our roots, once again becoming creatures motivated by our individual health and happiness rather than the norms imposed upon us by our society.

Flip Your Perspective

An inversion posture is any shape in which the heart is above the head or the legs are above the rest of the body in space. There are many different ways to invert the body, which range from easy to advanced in difficulty and from gentle to extreme in effect. I offer inverting as an essential healing concept instead of one specific shape. Like all the interventions offered in this book, beginning an inversion practice should be approached with caution. Wait until you know how well your body responds to gentler inversion shapes before trying more extreme variations.

Going upside down has many benefits similar to that of hanging, by altering how gravity affects the tissues, organs, and liquids of the body. Simply by laying down and lifting your legs up you flip the flow of fluids in your body as if upending an hourglass. Blood and lymph that have been struggling all day against gravity and the vessel valves to recirculate now flow naturally into the upper body. This increases the blood pressure in the upper body and decreases that of the lower body, sending more blood to the brain, heart, and other organs. Inverting allows the legs to decompress, aiding in relieving conditions associated with the veins of the legs and leg edema. Inversion therapy (to be discussed further later) utilizes this effect to help pass unwanted particles from the body such as fragments of kidney stones that have been broken up by percussion.[4]

More advanced inversion postures such as headstand and

handstand are useful for building a unique combination of strength, balance, confidence and coordination. In any inversion our perspective is flipped, both visually and in terms of vestibular perception. Many people report this shift in physical perspective creates a shift in their mental perspective. Seeing the world in a different way allows us to see ourselves and our problems in a different way, providing an opportunity to modify emotions. Perhaps this is a part of why inversions seem to have a calming effect on kiddos and adults alike.

Research suggests that regularly practicing inversion postures improves heart rate variability (HRV), the variation of time between heartbeats.[5] This variation is controlled by a primitive part of the nervous system called the autonomic nervous system (ANS). The ANS is constantly working to regulate our heart rate, blood pressure, breathing, and digestion, among other resting bodily functions. The ANS is divided into the sympathetic and the parasympathetic nervous systems. The sympathetic nervous system generates the fight-or-flight response, and the parasympathetic nervous system provides the relaxation response.

If you are chronically stuck in fight-or-flight, variation in the intervals between your heartbeats is low (low HRV). Your nerves are sending signals to the heart that it should remain prepared for action. A healthier system displays wider variations

Going upside down acts as a sensory reset which literally flips our perspective. For both adults and children this altered perspective is often quite soothing and has the power to shift our mood and help us process our emotions. This may be due to the effect inversions have on our autonomic nervous system.

in the intervals between heartbeats at rest. High HRV indicates that the body is capable of returning to a relaxed state after being exposed to a stressor and that the ANS is well balanced. The greater the health of your ANS, the faster you are able to switch gears from being aroused to relaxed, showing more resilience and flexibility to life's many hurdles.

Research has shown a relationship between low HRV and worsening depression or anxiety. Low HRV is also associated with an increased risk of early death from cardiovascular disease.[6] Many devices that started off as simple pedometers like Fitbits are now capable of monitoring HRV, offering us an easy and noninvasive way to monitor the health of the ANS. Newly designed smart watches and fitness trackers base their stress ratings and lifestyle change suggestions on HRV.

The fact that inverting regularly improves heart rate variability explains why yoga practitioners have been shown to have better vagal tone at rest compared to non-practitioners.[7] Vagal tone refers to the activity of the vagus nerve, a major player in the parasympathetic branch of the ANS. Vagal tone, as assessed by heart rate variability, can diagnose nervous system-related gut-brain disorders like inflammatory bowel disease. Preliminary evidence suggests that vagus nerve stimulation may also be an effective treatment for depression and PTSD.[8]

Inversion Therapy

The first inversion therapy was recorded in 400 BC, when the father of medicine Hippocratus strung up a patient by his legs via a system of pulleys and ladders to harness the healing power of gravity. Examples of more modern inverted exercises and equipment can be seen in the literature as far back as the 1800s. Utilizing an inversion apparatus is the most practical variation of inverting for clinical and therapeutic applications. This is because the sensation of reversing gravity's effect on the body can be edgy, but inversion devices help the invertee feel safer. They also make the inversion practice available to anybody, regardless of limitations.

Inversion therapy was popularized by Dr. Robert Martin and

his son Robert Martin, Jr., in the 1980s. It was during this time that inversion therapies went through a renaissance. The Martins released a system of inverted exercises and an apparatus for inverting oneself called "The Gravity Guiding System." This spurred on the invention of many other devices and therapies by doctors, healers, and fitness lovers all over the world. After The Gravity Guiding System was used by Richard Gere in the 1980 movie, *American Gigolo*, the system (and inversion therapy by proxy) gained widespread fame.

Many inversion apparatuses have since been utilized both clinically and recreationally, such as the Inverchair and various kinds of inversion tables. Extensive research has assessed the safety and effectiveness of these therapies and devices. Multiple studies have shown that inversion therapy reduces the need for surgeries prescribed to correct sciatica and lumbar degeneration by reducing the compressive force on the nerves and vertebral discs through traction.[9] Conditions like lumbar lordosis and thoracic kyphosis have also been recorded flattening out through regular inversion therapy. Most notably, a 2013 article in *Isokinetics and Exercise Science* concluded that inversion therapy was effective in relieving chronic low back pain, increasing spinal flexibility, and improving strength of the trunk muscles.[10]

Home inversion apparati should be used with caution. Extended bouts of inversion therapy have been shown to slightly increase fluid pressure in the eyes. Therefore, it should be avoided by people with glaucoma. It is also prudent to check with your doctor before starting inversion therapy or performing any intense inversion postures if you have been diagnosed with or could potentially have any condition of the heart, spine, eye or vestibular system. Again, the best plan of action if you are relatively healthy is to become proficient with gentle inversion shapes before attempting more extreme variations like those produced by home inversion devices.

Finally, a word on choosing the right inversion apparatus: Devices that suspend the body by the ankle joints such as common inversion tables are not ideal. Before starting my yoga journey, I had an inversion table for many years. It was helpful for relieving my back pain, but it also put unnecessary stress on my ankles and knees, predisposing me to tweaking and injuring these joints. Although children and our evolutionary ancestors hang/hung from their legs, this way of inverting involves strong muscular engagement that supports vulnerable joints, whereas inversion tables allow muscles and tendons to be passive.

Instead, I recommend devices that attach to the hips. These allow us to safely disengage into full relaxation in order to receive the most benefits with the least amount of risk. The hips and spine are resilient joints which are supported by more musculature, the passive tone of which supports them within traction, whereas knees and ankles are less receptive to this force. Most studies on the benefits of inversion therapy were done with devices like the Inverchair, which uses the thighs as the vector for hanging from. However, these devices are expen-

Inversion therapy has been used for thousands of years. This ancient practice utilizes an inversion apparatus to flip the patient upside down in order to generate spinal traction. Spinal traction creates space between the vertebrae, giving the nerves and discs a break from the compressive force of gravity. Common inversion tables make inversion therapy available outside of a clinical setting. However, these devices put stress on the vulnerable ankle and knee joints. Yoga swings and other devices that attach to the hips instead are safer and can be more affordable.

sive and not readily available, so I recommend a yoga swing or "silks," sturdy fabric hung overhead that encircles the hips to create the vector for inversion. I have also seen personal trainers utilize large resistance bands attached to a pull-up bar to create a similar shape with the added benefit of the pulling effect of the band.

Practice—Legs up the Wall

1. Sit in an "L" shape close to and parallel with a wall, tree, or piece of furniture with your legs outstretched in front of you.
2. Lie on your side away from the intended support, then turn to swing your legs up onto it. If you're placing your legs on something short like a chair or sofa, allow your legs to bend naturally at the knees. This will create a gentler inversion shape than legs vertical.
3. Remain here passively for as long as you feel safe. While you enjoy the stillness, notice the sensations that arise. Do your legs feel cooler or lighter? What happens to your perspective when you're looking up at the sky instead of staring down at the ground?

There are many ways to create an inversion effect in your body. Before exploring more intense inversion shapes, practice the basics. Legs up the wall, standing forward fold, and downward-facing dog are excellent introductions to the inversion effect. These gentler variations will prepare your body for more intense inversions like headstand and handstand.

12

Lying on the Ground (Savasana/Aomuke)

"Practice and all is coming."—Sri K. Pattabhi Jois

Benefits: *Promotes Relaxation, Decreases Blood Pressure, Improves Control of the Autonomic Nervous System, Increases the Effects of Exercise, Allows for Integration of Stressors, Reduces Fatigue, Regenerates Energy, Improves Sleep and Other Functions of the Parasympathetic Nervous System, Neutralizes the Body and Mind*
Counter Position: *Anything else*
Daily Goal: *As Long as You Like*

The final essential healing posture is the most passive of the eight as well as the most rejuvenating. It's the posture modern humans need most in their lives: lying on the ground. Reading this you might think, "finally, active rest means I get to take a nap!" But sleeping is not the same as lying down in active rest. Many yoga practitioners refer to savasana as the "hardest pose in yoga." This is because it asks us to do the opposite of what we are used to doing in day-to-day life. Instead of attempting to distract our busy minds with intense sensations, we are asked to simply lie down and do nothing. To use our mindfulness to create space within.

As a newcomer to yoga, I agreed with this label. Savasana always was the most challenging part of my practice during my teacher training. I was learning ashtanga yoga, a very vigorous style of yoga that lined up well with my hard-and-fast personality. The intense physical sensations distracted me from my inner workings. At the end of each practice, we would do a 20-minute relaxation practice lying on the ground. This is a very long relaxation by modern yoga class

Lying on the ground instead of on furniture encourages us to arrange our body in a way that is self-supportive. This keeps us in tune with our bodies, preventing us from remaining stagnant in one position too long like we might when sleeping on a memory foam mattress.

standards. My mind would race, my eyes would shoot open, and I felt as though I was missing the point. I asked my teacher if I was doing something wrong. Surely, I needed extra tutoring to master this relaxation posture. My teacher offered this: "Practice and all is coming." This was the first time I heard the infamous quote from the creator of ashtanga yoga, Pattabhi Jois. It is the same message that Dr. Sarno shares: That there is nothing wrong with us. All we need to do in order to heal is remove the myths of the mind and believe in our ability to overcome pain.

After a few weeks, the benefits of the posture started to reveal themselves to me. Since the movement practice was so intense, my body started to associate the contrast of lying motionless on the ground with a great release of effort. As I rested physically, my mind began to follow suit. If my eyes opened, I didn't consider it a problem. I could see more clearly the beauty of everything around me after my self-care practice. If thoughts came to my mind, I found a curiosity about them rather than a need to banish them. The uncomfortable thoughts about my past were just like uncomfortable physical sensations discovered in active yoga postures—something to work through but nothing to fear or avoid.

On the last day of my yoga teacher training I had a profound experience. Emotions were high in the yoga shala. We were all about to leave the paradise we had been practicing in for weeks and return to our busy lives back home. Yet there was also a sense of impending relief from the strict nature of our practices. We were eager to escape the harshness of the local climate and the discomfort of our rustic hostel rooms. Lying on the ground after our final practice, the woman next to me began to sob uncontrollably. She was very kind and supportive of me during the training, offering a maternal energy I found quite comforting. I realized through her kindness that I was missing that kind of support since the passing of my mother. I reached out and touched her hand as a sign of solidarity. She firmly squeezed my hand back, and suddenly I felt all of her emotions rush into me. I began to cry as well. I cried so hard and gutturally that it hurt like being punched in the stomach. I was purging something from within me that felt ancient.

I saw myself in a hospital intensive care unit, holding my mother's hand while she lay brain-dead on a bed next to me. It was minutes after we had agreed to remove her life support in order to respect her wishes to become an organ donor. It was a moment I hadn't allowed myself to think about in a long time. I remembered the sounds of my mournful wailing filling the unit, as if I were hearing them from outside my body. I was simultaneously feeling the anguish of my former self and the painful release I was having in the present moment. Although this experience was extremely uncomfortable, the catharsis was long overdue. I needed to let go and begin anew. In that moment, lying on the ground, I learned to stop pushing away the memories of all the people I had loved and lost in my life.

I snapped back to the present. My hand was now empty, and I was being given a savasana adjustment (much like a brief session of Thai massage) from my teacher. After he helped me calm down through loving touch, he sat beside me in silence for a moment before eventually encouraging me to sit up. "I can see them too," he said, meeting my tear-soaked eyes with an intense gaze. As a mist of emotion began to glaze his vision, he proclaimed, "You're ready to go home now."

Lay Down Your Weapons

When we lie on the ground, especially on a firm and flat surface within nature, we connect with one of the most instinctive and therapeutic forms of active rest. The stillness invites us to look upon ourselves in a way we cannot otherwise, by removing all of our distractions and returning our body and mind to neutral. We get the opportunity to integrate everything that has happened to us in the past with everything that is happening within us in the present. Seeing that we are safe in the present we can gradually begin to release our grip from the trauma we've trapped within us. We shed the armor we collected for protecting ourselves from our inner workings. We lay down the weapons we wield in our lives to fight off foes, real and imagined. In integrating our past and present selves, we see more clearly the path we wish to walk when we get up from the ground.

When an animal is seriously injured, it will focus all of its efforts towards self-healing through rest. It finds a safe place to lie down, even passing up opportunities to eat. When we are sick, we instinctively know the healthiest thing to do is to call out of work and curl up under the blankets. Instead, our society calls this instinct for self-healing weakness and discourages us from taking the rest time we need to recover.

The intention of savasana is not to fall asleep. However, it does improve our ability to fall asleep faster and increase the quality of our sleep.[1] With consistent practice,

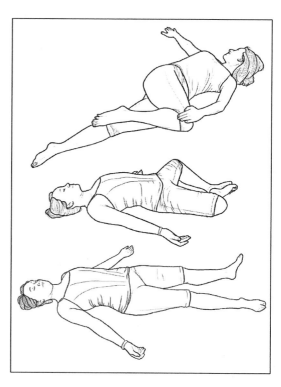

There are many stretches and other therapeutic exercises available while lying on the ground. Since it is in a position that induces relaxation, the body will associate the exercises with tranquility. This makes the exercises more effective and maintains a healthy balance of activity and rest.

152

incremental changes in our control over the autonomic nervous system accumulate, much like regular inversion practice. Lying on the ground while remaining present allows for powerful integration of all of your systems and all of your experiences. This can create a profound healing effect, like the one I experienced in my teacher training.

It's helpful to practice this pose after exercise. The contrast will help your body develop an association with the shift in shape to relaxation. Your body doesn't know the difference between running from a tiger, running around all day at work, and running on a treadmill. All increase your heart rate, breath rate, and production of stress hormones. Lying on the ground relaxing after any and all of these activities is beneficial. The more you repeat this practice, the more your body will automatically begin to relax upon visiting the ground.

If you lie on the ground after a workout or stressful event, you are training your body and mind to recover from stress more quickly. This will also give you an opportunity to enjoy all of the acute benefits of exercise, like the pharmacopoeia of natural pain relievers and antidepressants released in response to your workout. As the body begins to associate exercise with pain relief, antidepression, and relaxation, you will likely find more motivation for repeating the practice. Eventually, these positive associations become so strong that you will no longer need to exercise before lying on the ground to receive its relaxing benefits. Stretching is also safer and more effective after a workout. There are a multitude of relaxing and therapeutic stretches you can perform lying on the ground that speed recovery and help release excess tension.

Research indicates that combining exercise with meditation can improve blood pressure and recovery heart rate, and is an effective treatment for depression. One study compared the effects of blood pressure medication to 30 minutes of daily yoga. The yoga practice consisted of sun salutations (moderate intensity aerobic activity) followed by savasana. Results found that the yoga group and the drug group had similar reductions in blood pressure. The authors offer that the yoga practice is a safer alternative as it has no side effects. Another study asked participants to perform their meditation before exercising.[2] At the end of the eight-week intervention, subjects reported significant reduction in symptoms of depression.[3]

The benefits of lying on the ground are not dependent on exercise. Evidence suggests that hypertensive patients who regularly practice savasana have a notable reduction in blood pressure.[4] Findings from a study published in *Medical Express* indicate that practicing relaxation while lying on the ground "decreases cardiac sympathovagal balance in hypertensive

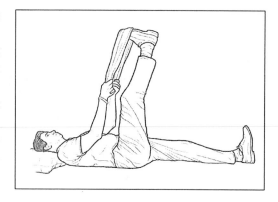

Stretching after exercise jump-starts the recovery process. Warm, blood-filled muscles stretch more effectively, aiding in the release of muscle tension. Endorphins released during exercise act as pain relievers, reducing the discomfort experienced while stretching.

patients." Risking oversimplification, cardiac sympathovagal balance could be explained as the balance between the effects of the sympathetic (fight or flight) and parasympathetic (relaxation response) nervous systems on the heart. Cardiac sympathovagal balance has been found to be a determinant of blood pressure variability. We want our blood pressure to vary throughout the day based on the demands of the body. If we exercise, blood pressure should increase. If we stop, it should decrease. Good blood pressure variability is considered a sign of resilience to stressors compared to chronically high blood pressure, an indicator of an overactive sympathetic nervous system. Hypertensive participants in the study who performed savasana showed significantly lowered cardiac sympathovagal balance during and maintained the benefits for 35 minutes after. The researchers hypothesize that hypertensive people lack the ability to decrease the sympathetic nervous system's influence on the heart and therefore focused periods of parasympathetic control like that found in savasana are helpful for retraining this function.[5]

Like the postures offered in the last two chapters, lying on the ground gains much of its effect from creating a shift in the way gravity affects the body. Instead of gravity compressing us as it does when seated or standing, gravity's downward pressure is dispersed evenly across our body. This even gravitational pressure created eases circulation and generates a sense of neutrality in the spatial senses.

It has been common for millennia for healers to prescribe lying on a hard flat surface to patients with deformed posture and various other ailments as they intuitively saw the benefits. When we lay flat, gravity helps our bodies settle into healthy alignment. The seesaw action of our inhales and exhales combined with gravity kneads our muscles and mind into letting go. Our bones sink to the earth, and space collects within the joints. If we are so fortunate to practice this posture in nature, its healing effects are multiplied exponentially, a phenomena to be discussed further in the following chapter.

Some contemporary healers and sleep specialists actually encourage sleeping on the ground, as is done traditionally in Japan and out of necessity in other places around the world. In his paper, "Instinctive sleeping and resting postures: an anthropological and zoological approach to treatment of low back and joint pain," physiotherapist Michael Tetly offers alternative sleeping shapes to bed rest:

> *I grew up with tribal people and in 1953–4 commanded a platoon of African soldiers from nine tribes, who taught me to sleep on my side without a pillow so that I could listen out for danger with both ears. I have organised over 14 expeditions all over the world to meet native peoples and study their sleeping and resting postures. They all adopted similar postures and exhibited few musculoskeletal problems. I must emphasise that this is not a comparison of genes or races but of lifestyles.*[6]

I wholeheartedly agree that overstuffed pillows and beds can cause us more pain than comfort, but I don't think it is necessary to burn your bed in order to receive the healing benefits of lying on the ground.

There are good reasons why humans began crafting elevated beds; uneven surfaces, pesky critters, and other hazardous elements make sleeping on the ground risky. But completely moving out of the natural world and removing instinctive ways of resting from our lives has disconnected us from our roots. Thankfully, reconnecting is simple, and the effects can be instantaneous. A few minutes of lying on the ground staring up at the clouds will shift your perspective and reestablish your connection to the healing energy of Mother Earth.

Practice—Lying on the Ground

1. Pick a place where you feel safe. Collect any items of support you may need: a mat, blankets, bolsters, etc. Be creative in building your nest, and remember that there's nothing wrong with adjusting after your practice has begun.
2. As you lie down, whether on your back or on your belly, notice what is comfortable and what is uncomfortable about this position. If you have an intuition that the discomfort you experience is therapeutic, consider staying with it and noticing how it evolves as you breathe.
3. Try on different angles of your arms and legs, and adjust the position of your head as needed. Generally speaking, straight lines or 90-degree angles at the joints will be more sustainable in most bodies, but every body is different. Only you will know what shape is right for your body and how long it is safe to be there.
4. Once you are relatively comfortable, begin to focus all of your attention towards your breath. When your mind drifts and thoughts don't feel useful, return your awareness to your breath. It may be helpful to focus on lengthening your exhale to encourage greater relaxation. You

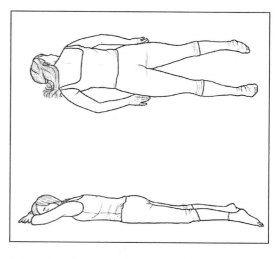

Lying face down on the ground has a calming effect because the pressure on our rib cage and abdomen encourages diaphragmatic breathing. Breathing deeply lying face down turns the diaphragm into a weightlifter when inhaling. When we exhale, the weight of the body helps squeeze the air out of the lungs, signaling the body to relax further.

12. Lying on the Ground (Savasana/Aomuke)

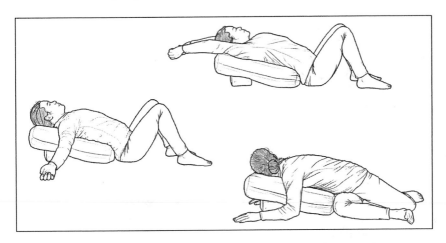

There are many ways to modify lying on the ground to create restorative shapes. In lieu of yoga props, use common household items like pillows, blankets, and books to build a nest for positions that offer gentle stretching and encourage deep relaxation. Lying with arms outstretched at different angles and arranging the legs in various ways will produce a wide array of sensations and benefits.

can also count the breath to anchor the mind, "In, two, three, four, five. Out, two, three, four, five." If you have the luxury of practicing in nature, extend your noticing out towards the elements. Feel the earth beneath you; smell the scents that surround you. Look deeply at the tree branches and clouds. Listen to far-off sounds as well as nearby ones. Welcome the touch of playful insects, healing rains, and cooling breezes. If you are inside or in an otherwise urban environment, use the sounds and other sources of stimulation around you as anchors to the present moment rather than labeling them distractions from your practice.

Sample Practice Plans for the Burn Your Chair Method

Now that you are familiar with the eight essential healing postures it is important to create a plan for your daily practice. This plan should reflect the needs of your body. The needs of your body are shaped primarily by lifestyle factors such as your profession, hobbies, and level of physical activity. It's pertinent to consider the history of your body and mind. Injuries and traumas you have experienced should be respected and addressed by your practice plan. Below are a few sample practice plans. They have been generalized towards specific populations. Use these practice plans as inspiration for building your own.

Practice Plan—Sedentary Desk Worker

1. Create a healing space at work. Of utmost importance is a standing desk. Also create space for shapes that counter standing such as sphinx pose and sitting on the ground. If getting onto the floor isn't possible at your workplace, use a stability ball to replace your chair.
2. Plan to spend as much of the day standing as possible, without being unkind to your body. Listen for body signals that warn you standing has gone on too long. When you receive such signals, cycle into an active rest shape that you are drawn to. Set a timer that goes off every half hour or hour. When it goes off, practice active rest postures or take a movement break. Go for a walk, hang, stretch, breath mindfully and practice a few therapeutic exercises like pelvic tilts. Whenever possible, take your movement breaks outside and consider bringing your workout with you.
3. Once you run out of energy for standing and movement breaks, start a seated practice. Use chairs sparingly, replacing them with active rest postures or alternative seats whenever possible. If you must sit in a chair, maintain a healthy foundation by tipping your hips forward, rolling your shoulders back, and maintaining an erect spine.
4. When you get home, do the opposite of whatever you spent most of your time doing at work. Avoid screens if you've been on the computer all day. Take more restful shapes that counter the effects of long periods of standing and sitting. Practice gentle inversions to relieve pressure from the lower body. Lay on the ground practicing mindful breathing for at least a few minutes before getting into bed.

12. Lying on the Ground (Savasana/Aomuke)

Practice Plan—Physical Laborer, High Activity Individual, or Athlete

1. Survey today's workspace for opportunities for active rest. Look for places to sit on the ground, things to support squatting, and overhead structures to hang from. Before engaging in strenuous activities, perform a thorough warm-up. One by one, move all of your joints in circles to lubricate them. Perform a few active rest shapes that speak to you the most, but don't hold them too long.

2. Plan to utilize active rest shapes as often as possible to facilitate the task at hand, but try not to overdo one posture. Be thoughtful of your movement patterns, keeping a neutral spine and engaged core. Pay close attention to the signals of your body, and respond accordingly. Your livelihood depends on it!

3. Take breaks from work as often as possible. If you are an athlete, resting in active shapes between sets or sprints is a good idea, but again, don't hold onto one shape too long. Overstretching diminishes your athletic potential.

4. When you get home at night, you may need to push yourself to slow down. If you need some kind of physical stimulation, lean towards passive rest activities like soaking in a bath or hot tub. If you are very sore, a brief ice bath or cold shower will ease your inflammation and quicken your time to recovery. Perform gentle active rest shapes like lying on the ground and legs up the wall before bed.

Practice Plan—Low/Moderately Active Individual with Time to Spare

1. Sculpt your space so that the needs of your daily life can be supported by active rest postures. Decide how you will perform hobbies and sedentary activities within these healing shapes. Consider how and when you want to perform your therapeutic exercise and active rest practices. Ideal options are in the morning (after your other needs are

taken care of), before lunch or bedtime, or intermittently throughout the day. This practice works best with the former two options.

2. After a few mindful breaths, perform a standing movement practice. Warm up by rolling each joint individually in circles; ankles, knees, hips, shoulders, and neck. Perform the six movements of the spine; bend side to side, flex and extend the back, and twist at the waist with arms to a T.

3. If you won't be able to go for a walk later, take one now. Go for as long as you like, performing the mindful walking practice from Chapter 9. Go barefoot if possible. If you don't walk now, consider performing therapeutic exercises instead.

4. Begin folding in active rest postures into your movement practice. This can be done on your walk, when you get back, or the end of your warm-up and other exercises. The order of the postures is not extremely important. It's more important to listen to your body for cues directing you how to complete the remaining shapes. However, the sequence to follow will create a chain of counter stretching.

5. Perform a hanging variation that works for you today. Work to complete your daily goal unless you plan to hang more later. This goes for all the remaining shapes.

6. Next, squat. If you need to take breaks but want to complete your daily goal, rest in a standing forward fold position. Or cycle into some of the other remaining shapes, and return to squatting later.

7. Place your hands on the ground, and walk them forward until you can come down to hands and knees. Rest your head on the ground, and stretch your arms out long, sitting your hips to your heels. Or perform another kneeling variation.

8. Once content with kneeling, lay down on your belly in sphinx pose.

9. From sphinx, transition either into sitting or lying on the ground. Perform a few stretches here before coming to stillness to practice mindful breathing for as long as you like.

10. When ready, assume an inversion shape that matches your

12. Lying on the Ground (Savasana/Aomuke)

experience and energy level. Alternatively, use a gentle inversion for your final relaxation posture.

11. Rest for as long as you like. If you haven't performed a lying down posture yet, use this for your final relaxation shape.

PART THREE

The World Is Your Yoga Mat

All of the practices offered in this book are *innate practices*. They are practices we were pre-programmed with in order to ensure our survival. Whether you are aware of it or not, you once naturally gravitated towards these practices. Given the opportunity, you performed them on instinct. No one had to teach you any of these shapes. You just did them because they felt right. Deep down, you still have this pull towards healthy practices. They are just harder to access because of the way you arrange your life. To break the cycle of pain, you need to remember who you once were. You need to reconnect with your roots.

There was a time when the eight essential healing postures were shapes you assumed out of instinct. You visited them for fun, to get something done, or to expel energy. You practiced them indoors and outdoors, in the presence of others and on your own. If you're reading this, it's likely that this is no longer the case. This means it's highly likely you are chronically overstressed, in constant pain, always getting sick, or all of the above. If so, now is the time to reintroduce the practices of your ancestors and your childhood back into your life.

This will be no small feat because the power of self-healing comes at a cost. To revitalize your self-healing capabilities you must demonstrate unwavering attentiveness to the needs of your body. You must become vigilant in warding off the trappings of modern life and return to a more natural existence. You must begin to see all things around you as useful, and look for places to insert your self-care practice. In the chapters to follow, you will learn ways to incorporate the teachings of this book into daily life.

In Part Three I will offer you ideas for rearranging your home and workspace in order to encourage the practice of active rest. Whether you live in the country or the city, your surroundings can support a self-care practice. You don't need a yoga studio or yoga teacher to find freedom within your body. In the chapters to follow you will meet the world's greatest yoga teachers and discover that they are far less strict and serious than you might think. Aided by the practices of your ancestors, your self-healing instincts, and a little help from Mother Earth, you will join the millions of people living pain-free lives all over the world.

13

Practicing in Nature

"The art of healing comes from nature, not from the physician."—Paracelcus

As you begin to weave the practice of active rest into your daily life, you may feel stifled by your surroundings. However, if you are looking deeply, you will notice that wherever you are, there is some way to utilize your surroundings for supporting your practice. The fact of the matter is, you are where you are. If you can't change the scenery, you can at least change the way you look at it. In the next two chapters, you'll learn why this shift in your thinking is so important. An open mind contains the power to make the world your yoga mat.

Reconnecting with the Earth— The Most Essential Healing Practice

Emerging research indicates that a myriad of health benefits are gained by touching, breathing in, listening to, or looking deeply upon nature. *Earthing* is the practice of connecting with the earth to tap into the healing power it holds. Regularly connecting to the earth attunes our bodies and minds to a more natural state of being. You may have noticed that warm sand beneath your feet feels soothing, gardening brings you peace and joy, and watching a beautiful sunset can reset your mood; that sitting next to a babbling brook washes out the sound of your mind, its cool water on your face feels invigorating, and watching the life contained within sparks a childlike curiosity in you. These healing sensations come from reconnecting with your natural roots.

Modern infrastructure, technology, and society are strong barriers between us and the natural world. Man-made structures and

screens obscure our view of natural surfaces and scenes. Even the clothes we wear and the food we eat have taken such great departures from their natural roots that we no longer know anything about them. Ask a child (or adult for that matter) where their food comes from or what it looks like in its natural state. Many will not have an answer. It is this kind of disconnect from the natural world that sparked the need for nature-based therapies and education. Earthing is a cornerstone self-healing practice to learn and relearn over the course of our lives now that modern life stands in our way of practicing it effortlessly as did our ancestors. There are two earthing practices that have gained notoriety worldwide as therapeutic modalities: *shinrin-yoku* and grounding.

It's no secret that touching, breathing in, and looking upon nature has a restorative effect. We all know the calm that comes when we go for a walk in the woods or lie down on the beach. Now science is beginning to explain why, providing evidence that suggests the practice of "earthing" can be profoundly healing for the body and mind.

Shinrin-Yoku (Forest Bathing)

Daily Goal: *15 Minutes or More*

Benefits: *Increases Immune Function, Improves Heart Rate Variability, Improves Mood and Positive Thinking, Increases Activity*

13. Practicing in Nature

of Anticancer Proteins, Decreases Stress Hormone Production, Improves Pulse Rate, Reduces Inflammation, Reduces Hypertension, Reduces Markers of Cardiovascular Disease

In 1982, the Forest Agency of Japan introduced the practice of shinrin-yoku, which literally translated means "forest bathing" or "taking in the forest atmosphere" as a means to improve public health. Practitioners walk mindfully through natural spaces and explore the effects of connecting with the earth. They look deeply at the beauty of the scenery, listen closely to the sounds of animals and the environment, touch natural surfaces with bare skin, take in earthy smells, and even taste bits of edible plants and soils.

Human physiology evolved in attunement with the natural world. Artificial environments are inherently stressful unless they are mindfully constructed and organized. With this in mind, there should be little surprise that shinrin-yoku has been proven to offer modern bodies healing effects.

Since its introduction in the '80s, the practice of forest bathing has seen measured success, inspiring scientists to ask, "Why?" and "How could this be clinically applied?" The answers found have been astounding, as the list of benefits above demonstrates. Researchers began examining the obvious and immediate effects of shinrin-yoku such as stress relief and improved sleep. As they dug deeper, they found that forest bathing is an effective prevention modality for some of the deadliest conditions known to modern man.

Perhaps the most fascinating discovery is that airborne phytoncides (wood essential oils) present in forest air increases the activity of our natural killer (NK) immune cells. NK cells have the ability to release anticancer proteins, to control microbial infections, and to modulate overactive or underactive immune responses. Multiple studies have demonstrated this effect and compared it to the effects of living in urban environments. Urban air contains little to no phytoncides and instead assaults the body with pollution. One study reported that improvements in the immune system were still present up to a week after returning to an urban environment.[1,2]

An article published in the *Journal of Cardiology* demonstrated the value of shinrin-yoku in reducing hypertension in elderly subjects.

After a seven-day forest bathing journey, participants showed significantly reduced blood pressure compared to the control group who went on holiday in a city. Cardiovascular disease markers and inflammatory proteins were also measured. The city group showed little to no change in these factors, whereas the forest group showed significantly reduced CVD and inflammatory markers. Most notable were markers demonstrating inhibition of the body's renin-angiotensin system, which plays a critical role in the development of visceral obesity and metabolic disorders.[3]

Taking in the forest atmosphere (a practice known as "forest bathing") has a profound meditative effect. Research indicates that forest bathing has a strong effect on our immune system. Airborne tree essential oils ramp up the activity of our natural killer cells, encouraging the release of anticancer proteins. Combining the practices of forest bathing, active rest and mindful breathing creates a powerful cocktail of self-healing benefits.

Finally, a study that deserves special note: In 2018 Bielinis et al. measured the effects of winter forest bathing on 62 young adults. Subjects were either exposed to a "city forest" or an urban control environment for 15 minutes. Before and after exposure, participants filled out surveys on their sense of self and mood. Results found that exposure to the city forest significantly increased positive scores and decreased negative scores compared to the urban control group.[4] This means that the healing effects of nature are available within urban environments if they contain natural elements even on bleak winter days. Nature can heal us anytime, anywhere.

The practices of active rest and forest bathing amplify each other. Try the practice on for yourself, walking mindfully through natural environments or assuming active rest postures supported by nature. Aim for an exposure of at least 15 minutes a day, bearing in mind that these practices are cumulative, so this prescription should be considered the bare minimum.

Practice—Shinrin-Yoku

1. Enter a natural environment, preferably a forest or another space rich with flora.
2. As you walk or practice active rest postures, slow yourself down by focusing on your sensations.
3. Look deeply. Focus on signs of life in fine detail. Then broaden your perspective to visually embrace the horizon.
4. Listen deeply. Hear the sounds of your footfalls. Notice the sound of your breath, or if you're still enough, the sound of your heart. Listen for sounds close to you and far away from you. Hone in on natural sounds like birds chirping and branches blowing in the breeze.
5. Touch deeply. Run your hands across the bark of a tree. Touch soft plants and smooth stones. Embrace the earth with bare feet.
6. Breathe deeply. Take in the rich smells of the earth, plants and animals. Fill your lungs with the healing particles contained in forest air.
7. Taste safely. Bring a field guide or an educated friend to help you forage for edible plants or to identify edible soils. Expand your palette by tasting the complexity of uncultivated foods.

For a guided forest bathing meditation, visit the bonus resource guide at *www.burnyourchair.com*.

Grounding

Daily Goal: As Long as Possible

Benefits: Improves Sleep, Reduces Inflammation, Reduces Oxidative Stress, Stabilizes Bioelectrical Body Systems, Reduces Blood Viscosity, Regulates Endocrine and Nervous System Functions, Improves Vagal Tone, Improves Immune Health, Quickens Wound Healing, Reduces Muscle Soreness

Free radicals are unstable molecules that are produced in the body naturally as a byproduct of metabolism. Exposure to toxins such as ultraviolet light and tobacco smoke increase free radical formation, but so does exercise. Free radicals contain an unpaired electron that attacks important macromolecules in our body, leading to oxidative stress, cell damage, and inflammation. The most debilitating diseases faced today and the aging process are caused by or associated with chronic inflammation and oxidative stress. Luckily, planet Earth is like a giant bioelectric battery, the surface of which is brimming with free electrons donated by millions of daily lightning strikes and constant solar radiation. When we become *electrically grounded* by making skin-to-earth contact, these free electrons move into our body and neutralize free radicals.

Around the turn of the 20th century, the rubber sole shoe was introduced by the US Rubber Company, sparking huge demand and production. For all of human existence before the shoe, we were regularly coming in direct skin-to-earth contact. Even leather moccasins, which have been worn for more than 14,000 years, are conductive when moistened by sweat or dew. Some pain specialists refer to the common shoe as "the world's most dangerous invention," as it separates us from the natural healing power contained in planet Earth. This is because the rubber sole shoe is a strong insulator that stops us from becoming electrically grounded through contact with the earth. Our cars, roads and homes also insulate us from the conductivity of the Earth. This is a dangerous recent phenomenon because our bioelectric bodies evolved to function optimally while grounded.

Being chronically disconnected from the earth leaves us in a state of electrical imbalance that leads to pain and disease. We wouldn't build a house without connecting it to a ground rod because power surges and lightning strikes could fry our electrical components or even burn the house down. Why then would we choose to live ungrounded in our bodies, leaving our internal electronics vulnerable and our bodies burning from inflammation?

Grounding your body is easy. Simply slip your shoes off, and touch your bare skin to the earth. The most conductive surfaces are grass, dirt, and rock. Wet surfaces are more conductive than dry, and saltwater is more conductive than fresh. The practices of grounding, forest bathing and active rest combine easily to create a deeply healing practice. If walking with bare feet is dangerous in your environment, touch any other part of your skin to safe spots on the ground or conductive materials that are in contact with the earth for the same effect.

Dozens of research papers have been produced in regards to grounding (sometimes synonymously referred to as "earthing") in the past few decades. Authors of a recent review of the literature on grounding published in *Alternative Therapies* proclaim that grounding provides us "electric nutrition," voltaic food for our heart, brain, immune and endocrine systems, all of which are regulated by bioelectric signals:

> *Electrons from Earth serve as a potent neutralizer or quencher of electron-seeking free radicals. The term "electron deficiency" may be appropriate to describe the largely ungrounded status of most of humanity. As noted, the modern lifestyle, notably the wearing of shoes with synthetic soles, has severed us from our electric roots, our connection with Earth and its natural supply of electrons.*

Culling information from more than 12 peer-reviewed research studies, the authors highlighted these six effects: reduced inflammation and pain, improved blood flow and reduced blood viscosity, reduced stress, better sleep, improved energy, improved response to trauma and injuries and accelerated wound healing.[5]

Walking barefoot is an ancient practice that keeps us in contact with the Earth. While connected to the Earth, our body is electrically grounded. "Grounding" neutralizes free radicals in our bodies that would otherwise cause excessive inflammation and suppress our ability to self-heal.

There are additional studies on the effect grounding has on wound healing that support its use for athletics and human performance. These studies

171

measured delayed onset muscle soreness (DOMS) as the experimental injury. DOMS is that deep discomfort you feel in your legs after running for the first time in months or hitting it hard at the gym. It sneaks up on you after as long as 48 hours, leaving you walking like a zombie and thinking, "What did I do?" A study published in *The Journal of Alternative and Complementary Medicine* found that participants who were grounded after a workout that induced DOMS reported reduced pain as well as reduced markers of muscle damage and inflammation compared to those who were "sham grounded."[6] Another study from *Frontiers in Physiology* echoed these results, reporting that their grounded group maintained higher red blood cell concentrations and showed lower inflammation markers than did the control group.[7] A synonymous study published in the *Open Access Journal of Sports Medicine* repeated similar results as well. Grounding significantly increased platelet count in the blood and reduced loss of creatine kinase in the injured muscles, indicating reduced muscle damage.[8] These studies indicate that grounding is an essential part of any athlete's recovery program.

But you don't need to be an athlete to benefit from grounding. In one of the most groundbreaking studies on earthing to date, researchers from the Division of Newborn Medicine at Penn State Children's Hospital in Hershey, Pennsylvania, examined the effect of grounding preterm infants. Medical scientists wanted to study the effects of grounding on vagal tone, an indicator of full-term survival. Based on the elevated floating skin voltage of their tiny patients, they theorized that incubators and other electrical equipment present in modern NICUs create a hostile electrical environment and that grounding could potentially alleviate the negative effects.

The results are remarkable. Almost instantaneously from being attached to a grounded electrode, floating skin voltage of the infants dropped by an astonishing 93 percent. Grounding also coincided with a 67 percent increase in vagal tone as measured by heart rate variability, an effect which disappeared after removing the grounded electrode. The researchers concluded, "The electrical environment affects autonomic balance. Grounding improves vagal tone and may improve resilience to stress and lower the risk of neonatal morbidity in preterm infants."[9] This evidence indicates that it may be possible to protect ourselves from electrically hostile environments such as hospitals, airports, and the office through indoor grounding devices.

Most grounding studies utilize artificial connections to the Earth's surface to ground participants because it's less complicated than getting them to maintain contact with the Earth. Conductive mats, bracelets, or sheets that are connected to the ground port of common electrical outlets are now widely available to the public. Other grounding devices connect to a dedicated ground rod that is buried in the earth. My favorite grounding products are listed in the *Burn Your Chair* bonus resource guide at *www.burnyourchair.com.* Grounding products are helpful healing tools when you are forced to spend long periods of time disconnected from the Earth, like when you're at work or in bed. However, I believe that the effects of grounding are exponentially increased when we directly touch the earth with our skin. This cuts out the middleman, reducing what some scientists refer to as "ground resistance," while also combining the effects of grounding with that of *shinrin-yoku.* So whenever possible, get outside to reconnect. There you'll rediscover the healing power of our home planet.

Grounding the human body may be "the most important health discovery ever," a claim made by Clint Ober, earthing pioneer in the subtitle to his book *Earthing.*[10] It's a claim that is resounded by scholars, scientists, and doctors who all endorse the benefits of earthing. It is vitally important to public health that this healing practice become common knowledge.

Combining the practices of active rest and grounding is easy. Simply perform active rest postures barefoot on natural surfaces. If being barefoot isn't comfortable, you can wear leather moccasins or wool socks since they are conductive when moistened by dew or sweat. You can also become grounded by touching the Earth (or other conductive surfaces that are in contact with it) with your hands or other bare skin.

Practice—Grounding

1. Stand or walk barefoot on naturally conductive surfaces such as soil, sand, grass, gravel, or rock. Avoid asphalt, vinyl, rubber and wood when attempting to ground, as these are not conductive surfaces.

2. If touching the earth with your feet is too much of a hassle, use your hands or other bare skin to connect. Place your hands on the ground in a squat, or hang from metal monkey bars that are rooted in the earth. If grounding outside is unavailable or unsafe, use a grounding product instead. Make sure the outlet you connect your product to is properly grounded by using a ground reader.

3. Pay attention to your body closely as you go from being ungrounded for long periods of time to becoming grounded. Are there any noticeable acute effects? After long periods of consistent grounding, what do you notice?

14

Practicing in
Urban Environments

*"A city always contains more than any inhabitant can
know, and a great city always makes the unknown and
the possible spurs to the imagination."*
—Rebecca Solnit

When nature is not available to you, it is still possible to utilize your environment to support self-healing. There are many structures in urban settings that are useful for self-care, some of which are also electrically grounded. Parks and other greenspaces can act as oases of natural healing energy within the urban desert. In this chapter, I'll share with you some of my favorite ways to practice in urban environments. However, it is far more important to use your imagination and consider your individual needs than it is to follow in my footsteps. Just remember that everything is useful, and the city will become your yoga mat.

You are bound to receive some strange looks as you practice, especially in inner cities. When you squat beside a perfectly good bench or sit on the floor beside a perfectly good chair, people will be puzzled and sometimes even offended. If you encounter these social edges, it's important to remind yourself that you are pushing against convention. You are rebelling against the idea that fitting in means accepting pain and disease. Along with the "Wow, what a weirdo" looks you might get, you will also notice the "Ooh, that looks like it feels good, I should try that" looks. Or, better yet, without saying anything, some people will move into their own instinctive practice inspired by your bravery. You'll find deep satisfaction when others join you in stretching, kneeling, and self-healing. Soon your

175

peaceful message of self-care will spread to others like an infectious smile.

It's a very modern practice to put formalities and social status higher on the priority list than well-being. This transforms our homes, offices, and communal spaces into painful prisons for our bodies and minds. Afraid of what others might think we sit in unforgiving plastic chairs rather than arrange our bones in a way that is truly comfortable. Afraid for our safety, we're unlikely to walk barefoot in the park or lay on the ground to stare up at the stars. If even just a few of us were brave enough to stand up to the social confines that cause us pain, perhaps sweeping societal change could ensue that will lead to the end of the age of chronic pain.

With playful exploration you will discover that urban and indoor environments can be as useful as natural ones. Every surface and structure can become companions to your daily practice of self-care. I started writing this book just as I embarked on a road trip across the United States. I was a country boy in search of an inspiring city to settle in one day. At first, daily self-care on the road seemed impossible. It was the middle of winter, and there was little room for movement in my small RV. The ceilings were too low and the walls too close together.

As I made my way through the southern states, my perspective shifted. I witnessed the unforgiving poverty plaguing our country that is more easily hidden up north where I'm from. My small RV began to feel like a palace. It dawned on me how lucky I was to have a tiny home. Suddenly I had an epiphany—it was only my mind stopping me from taking care of myself, not the walls I was so fortunate to have surrounding me.

Soon I began practicing in my RV anytime the weather conditions weren't ideal. I adapted my movements to the small space. I used the ceiling, the table, the bed, and every other available surface for supporting my practice. I discovered that if I maintained an open mind and playful spirit, the walls around me didn't stifle my practice. On the contrary, they were extremely useful for deepening it. I discovered new movements, stretches, and ways of supporting myself that I may have never noticed in a wide-open space.

Inspired by this, I challenged myself to make the best out of the suffocating surroundings I discovered within urban environments while traveling. On public transit, I never fought for a seat. Instead I looked for the part of the bus or subway car that had the best variety of handrails, as they offered me so many opportunities for self-care. I hung on overhead handles, performed standing stretches, or squatted against a wall to make room for someone else. Waiting in long lines for food or attractions gave me plenty of time to stretch after walking for hours.

Initially, my yoga practice started and ended on the mat. I thought that the healing power of yoga was limited to the rectangular piece of rubber under my feet. It's ironic to realize now that my yoga mat was actually insulating me from being electrically grounded, disconnecting me from powerful healing energy. Yet even before learning about the benefits of earthing, I began to notice that my practice

Practicing active rest in urban environments is easy because there are so many possibilities all around you. You can inconspicuously hang from safety handles, squat with your back to a wall, or perform simple seated stretches when it's impossible to avoid chairs.

felt stifled by this small piece of padding. More and more I decided to leave my mat behind. As I stretched my stance out wider than my yoga mat allowed, I felt an intuition that the shapes were best practiced in direct contact with the environment. It just felt right. My practice was deepened tenfold when practicing on the grass, in the sand, on concrete, or in a small mobile home.

Below are a few ideas of how you can utilize structures that are common in urban environments for supporting your practice. But remember, the real change happens in your mind. When you open up your creative instincts and discover your own unique healing path, you are no longer limited by experience or environment. There are infinite ways in which what's possible in your body can be changed by the support of your environment.

1. **Doors:** Chances are you pass through dozens of doors each day. Each time you do so, you are presented with a structure that can aid you in self-care. It's a bit too much to stop and stretch in each one, but if you pause in every second or third door, your practice will benefit greatly. Grip the outer edges of the door frame and lean forward to stretch your chest. Grip the top of the door frame and bend your legs to create traction in your shoulders. If it's appropriate, lie down within the door, perpendicular to the wall, and stretch a leg straight up one side of the door frame with the other leg on the ground for a deep hamstring stretch. These exercises are also aided by pillars, posts, walls and other structures you encounter throughout your day.

2. **Stairs:** Sometimes stairs may seem like a hurdle to climb. Perhaps the next time you come upon a staircase you can look at it differently. Stairs are a wonderful surface to stretch and rest on because there are many levels to modify your postures with. For instance, if you can't touch the ground in a forward fold, stand in front of the stairs and place your hands on one that is within reach. For tight calves, grip the railing and stand on a step with your toes on the edge and your heels hanging off. To open your hips, sit on the second or third step and cross one leg over the other in a figure-four shape, and then lean forward over your legs. If you have trouble squatting,

sit on one stair with your legs arranged below in a squatting shape.

3. **Chairs:** No matter how hard we try to avoid it, chances are we'll be forced to sit in a chair at some point during the day. If we are dedicated to the idea, "everything is useful," we can see that even chairs can aid in deepening our practice. In fact, chairs have been making yoga and fitness available to injured and aged bodies for many years. Seated in a chair there are a multitude of twists, folds, and side stretches available. A sturdy chair is also a great support for standing exercises and balancing postures, as well as the perfect prop for a gentle inversion.

With commitment to self-care and willingness to explore, there is no structure or situation that will offer you anything less than

Indoor environments offer a wide array of tools for enhancing your self-care practice. With a little imagination, everything around you can become useful. Stairs offer varying heights that can make stretches and exercises more or less challenging depending on your needs. Doors offer us the opportunity to simulate hanging or otherwise stretch the upper body. Even chairs can sometimes offer us more mechanical advantages than sitting on the ground for deepening the practice of active rest.

everything you need. For more ideas on practicing in metro environments, look to the urban acrobats of your city. The parkour punks who have apelike agility swinging from structure to structure. The skater kids who perform impressive tricks and float effortlessly across the pavement. The yogis who levitate into handstands in the park. They haven't allowed their surroundings to stifle their potential, why should you? Look at the things that surround you with the curiosity and playfulness of a child. Soon your environment will begin to speak to you and become the inspiration for a lifelong practice of self-care.

If you are clever and observant, you can find time for active rest in-between or within all of your daily activities. I call this practice *the twofer,* as in two for one. The twofer can be utilized in all areas of your life, not just your stretching practice. It has the potential to heighten awareness, prevent boredom, and make more efficient use of your time. The idea is to find activities that will benefit from or be enhanced by other activities when done together.

Incorporate active rest into your day any time you have to wait. Waiting in line, for the bus, or at the doctor's office, simple standing and chair-based stretches help pass the time in a therapeutic way. At the airport most people congregate in seating areas or stand frozen in lines long before their planes have arrived. This leaves plenty of space for sitting on the floor with your back to a wall so you can safely stretch before an agonizing eight hours strapped to a seat. If you're working from home, put your laptop on the floor so you can lie in a sphinx pose to read another long article or send emails. Where other people stand rigid or sit uncomfortably in chairs, you can utilize active rest to make more efficient use of your time.

Active rest can enhance other activities. Instead of sitting, reclining, or lying on furniture, practice active postures while you read, write, work on the computer, or watch TV.

Practice—Two for One

1. Consider some activities you do regularly. Focus on activities you "could do with your eyes closed" or that don't require your undivided attention.
2. Experiment with different ways of utilizing active rest to make these activities a twofer. Maybe you play with balancing on one foot while washing the dishes or use the toilet to create a standing lunge stretch when brushing your teeth.
3. Notice if these activities are made better by heightened awareness of your body. If the time you spend waiting seems to go by more quickly, if mundane tasks feel more fun, or if you can successfully complete two chores at once, you've found yourself a twofer!

Case Study—Kirsten

My online client, Kirsten, likes to practice in her room because it is a safe haven of privacy and quiet in her shared space. During our first session, it was clear that her room also made her feel a bit boxed in. Kirsten's practice seemed limited by the small space and its clutter. Through the computer screen, I peered into her life and looked closely at what was around her.

"What about that shelf behind you?" I asked her. "Can you use it to support you in this stretch?" Her eyes lit up at the possibility. She stretched her arms out and grabbed the edge of the shelf and leaned back to simulate hanging. The rest of her session utilized the bed, closet, and window for deepening her practice. As we debriefed after the session, I asked her what it was like to use her surroundings for deepening her practice.

"I feel much more comfortable in my room now," she replied, "and that means a lot to me because I really need this safe space." What Kirsten discovered was the beauty that was surrounding her for years. All she needed was a new perspective, and suddenly everything was useful.

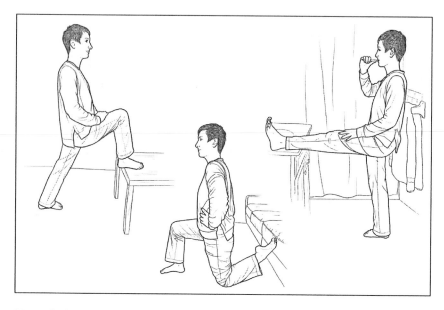

Household items and furniture transform when you stop looking at them as single-use items and start being creative in utilizing them to promote the practice of active rest.

Barriers to Change

Many modern cultures contain painful codes of conduct that adults are expected to follow in order to be considered "normal." It's considered impolite or immature to be playful, to take up space, or to otherwise go against the grain. Of course there are rules that keep people safe which we should accept and follow, like driving on the right side of the road. But keeping up appearances shouldn't come at the cost of our well-being. When you practice self-care in public, social barriers may affect your practice. It's edgy for others to see you be true to yourself when they're still stuck in their disguise. Reactions will range from confused looks from strangers to annoyance from friends. Some will view it as a distraction or an insult if you choose to sit on their floor instead of their expensive furniture. It's helpful to let people know right away that you like to sit on the floor. Explain that you are exploring active rest as a lifestyle, and invite them to join you if they seem curious.

You could also compliment your host's space and specifically their floor if you intend to use it. Just like you might coo in pleasure and remark how comfortable their antique fainting couch is, you can also compliment the softness of their carpet or the craftsmanship of their hardwood floor. If sitting on the floor is too much for the crowd you're with, another solution is to find less obvious ways to practice from the seat you're offered. Find active shapes that you can do while sitting on a couch or recliner. Be mindful of your posture while sitting. This will allow you to be more present and appear more alert while also remaining attentive to the needs of your body.

It may not always feel comfortable or appropriate to incorporate the ideas offered in this book into your public life. In those moments, consider how you will find time later to connect with your body. The world of chairs and car rides does not have to be a prison nor does it have to be something we fight against or refuse to accept. We can be in harmony with all things, even the chairs. All it takes is maintaining the free spirit and open-mindedness of our inner child and the resolve to protect ourselves from preventable chronic pain.

15

Creating a Healing Space

"We shape our dwellings, and afterwards, our dwellings shape us."—Winston Churchill

Up until this point I have encouraged you to make the best of your surroundings without resisting them. Whenever possible, it is also important to shape your surroundings in order to cultivate the kind of energy you want in your life. In this chapter you will learn how to create a healing space in your workplace, at home, or anywhere else you choose to practice. At work, a healing space ensures you can practice all day. By creating spaciousness at home, your family will feel free and you will experience a more easeful flow to life.

Make Your Workplace a Healing Space

Let's face it, work is often a place we derive much of our stress, bad habits, and pain from. This is why it is a vital practice to make your workplace a healing space. If you have your own workstation, customizing it to protect your body and encourage your practice is easy. Of vital importance is a standing desk of some kind. If you cannot afford a full standing desk, there are tabletop standing desks available that sit on an already established surface and raise up to chest height. These standing desks are my favorite because, unlike a full sit-stand workstation, they are portable. They can follow you down to the ground when you tire from standing or go outside with you when the weather permits. For a list of my favorite standing desk products, visit the *Burn Your Chair* bonus resource guide at *www.burnyourchair.com*. But you don't have to wait for your

184

standing desk to come in the mail before you modify your workspace for active rest. For the longest time I used a few cardboard boxes for my standing desk, and that worked just fine.

If you work indoors, it's imperative that you practice earthing throughout your day. Place a grounding mat below your feet or under your keyboard. Take regular breaks to walk outside and breathe fresh air. Put a potted plant or fresh-cut flowers on your desk. Use a light therapy box to simulate the sun's healing rays, or position your desk so that you can see out the window.

Stock your workplace with healing items. In place of a grounding mat any anti-fatigue mat or otherwise cushy surface can protect your feet for a few more minutes of stand time. A blow-up stability ball can replace a chair when standing is no longer available and sitting on the ground doesn't feel doable. Blankets and pillows may seem like they're meant for the bedroom, but comforting yourself with them throughout the day is a great way to encourage active rest. You'll learn more about the use of healing items later in this chapter.

If you work a job that does not have you sitting or standing still for long, you can still incorporate active rest into your workday. For instance, a cook who has to bend over many times a day to pick up plates has the opportunity to practice good

The standing desk is an essential item for practicing active rest while working. Paired with a stability ball for short bouts of sitting, the standing desk converts your workstation from a place of painful postures to a space of fluid movement.

squat form and hip hinging often. A carpenter who has to get down on the ground to measure, cut and nail down flooring can squat, kneel, and sit on the ground depending on which posture best complements the task at hand.

Look at the items specific to your trade for supporting your practice of self-care. Use your broomstick to help stretch your arms. Step one leg up on your desk to stretch your legs. Use the steps to your office to stretch your calves. Whatever your profession is, there are ways in which you can incorporate your body's innate ability to self-heal into your workday. If your boss has a problem with it, remind them that a happy and healthy worker is one who calls out less and produces more. Whatever you do, don't let your job be the reason that you are always sick, permanently deformed, or in constant pain.

Give Your Family the Gift of Spaciousness

Families that develop in confined, cluttered, and chaotic households inevitably become dysfunctional. Research indicates that children who grow up in "low-quality homes" are more likely to be chronically stressed. Factors such as poor air quality, noise, and lack of access to outdoor spaces lead to dysregulation of children's neuro-endocrine and immune systems. Obesity, socioemotional issues, and cognitive problems are common for kids living in these conditions.[1] Marriages and partnerships will similarly struggle to find the healthy foundation necessary to grow upon if their home base is a source of chaotic energy. Cultivating spaciousness in our homes gives our family the life they deserve. Little changes in how you clean and organize your space and the items you choose to keep around will create big changes in your life.

Spaciousness can be defined as a "lack-there-of," the void in which all things exist. Living in spaciousness aids in development, increases productivity, and alleviates anxiety and depression. When people enter spacious environments, they grow right before your eyes. They become more expressive and authentic because they feel free to take up more space. Research indicates that abundant space found in lush natural environments increases feelings of joy in children and adults alike. Given the choice, people naturally gravitate to these places.[2]

When you fold up your dining room table to make room for your children to play, you are giving them the gift of spaciousness. When you collect your tools into an empty crate so that there is more room for your spouse to park in the garage, you are giving her the gift of spaciousness. When you clean up, minimize your belongings, or take out the trash, you are giving your family the gift of spaciousness. Given this gift, you will see your family blossom. Your children will feel encouraged to sprawl out on the floor to read or color. Your partner will be more productive as he works around the house and feel more rejuvenated by the active rest that is available in your home. Your guests will be more comfortable when they come over for a visit

Children need space to grow. In environments devoid of space, children feel suffocated, leaving them in a state of chronic stress that stifles their development. By decluttering your home and taking your children outside often, you give them spaciousness they need to develop naturally and thrive.

since you have so much space to share. Even if your home is small, there are many ways to create spaciousness within it, such as utilizing variable furniture.

Cultivating spaciousness in your home will encourage you and your family to live exuberantly and to rest actively. Your home will be a place to recharge and an example of quality living that will radiate to your friends and community.

The Developing Family and Their Need for Space

Humans are largely a product of their environment. Children are particularly susceptible to the influence of their environment and how they see adults behave. Given the space, most children will automatically assume the eight essential healing postures. If you choose to model these active rest postures through your own daily practice, they will become solidified in your children's habits. If you make practicing active rest a daily family tradition, the habit will become permanently ingrained. Cultivating spaciousness at home offers your children the freedom to naturally develop a lifelong practice of self-care that will give them a life free from pain.

As children grow and spend more time at school, the pressures of society will begin to encroach. Their friends and teachers will tell them to conform. When this happens, continue compassionately encouraging them to be themselves and to stay connected with their bodies. Long hours sitting at desks can quickly turn into physical dysfunction. If you remain steadfast in modeling the practice of active rest, your children will maintain healthy habits they can turn to when times are tough.

If you have the option, consider enrolling your children in nontraditional schools that embrace these values and practices. Nature-based education is emerging from the wake of uncertainty left behind by the COVID-19 pandemic as a safer and more holistic option. Learning in the "invisible classroom" nurtures connection with nature, allows more explorative educational opportunities to occur, and encourages healthy instincts like active rest. If nature-based education isn't available to your family, consider lobbying your school board to offer more time for recess and physical education or to install standing desks. All of these things will improve the health of students, increase their ability to focus, and help them learn better. If money is a barrier for your school, help organize a fundraising committee.

Feng Shui *and the Flow of Your Space*

The ancient Chinese developed *feng shui* as a way of organizing their homes, businesses, and communities to optimize the flow of *ch'i* (life energy) around them. Proper *feng shui* in your home or workplace will encourage the spaciousness that is necessary to bring healing into your life. Here are five basic ways you can utilize *feng shui* to improve the flow of life energy in your space:

1. ***The Joy of Tidying Up:*** Begin your *feng shui* practice by carefully considering each item in your home and whether or not it brings you true joy. Do the items in your home create the kind of energy you want in your life? Do they support your practice? If the answer is "no" or "I'm not sure," give them away to someone who needs them more than you or recycle them. Purging unnecessary items from your home will feel cleansing. It can also be hard work that feels like grueling therapy, so take your time, perhaps resolving to give away one unnecessary item each week until you're left only with things that are truly useful and enriching to your life.

2. ***Invite in the Natural World:*** Our bodies run more efficiently when supplied with adequate oxygen and natural light. Whenever possible, invite the natural world into your space. Open the windows so fresh air can circulate in. Keep the blinds open to stay connected with the light patterns of day and night. Bring in potted plants and fresh flowers to clean the air. The closer you live to the natural world and its patterns, the more in sync and balanced you will feel.

3. ***Clear Path, Slow Energy:*** In *feng shui* great emphasis is placed on making clear paths for energy to flow easily, as well as creating reasons for energy (and people) to slow down. A simple example is the front door, which is an important

energy portal. The path leading to your front door and from the door into your space should be clear, well-marked, and inviting. A piece of art, flowers, a mirror or a statue that catches the eye upon entering will invite a healthy pause. Hang photos that ascend staircases with you. Remove any obstacles or tripping hazards from the floor, especially in hallways or on staircases. In large spaces or long paths, place an area rug or runner to add texture and color without taking up space. If something makes it hard to move about your space, remove it, and if your home feels too fast and open-ended, strategically place items that slow down the energy.

4. *Protect the Healthy Trinity:* There are three places in your home that are inextricably connected to your health: the kitchen, the bathroom, and the bedroom. It is impossible to expect optimum health if we don't protect the healthy trinity. Fill your kitchen with foods that feed both heart and soul. Clean regularly so that cooking surfaces aren't breeding grounds for bacteria. Keep your bathroom hygienic and free of clutter. Your bedroom should be a place that is welcoming each time you return to it. Vacuum, sweep, and change your linens often to allow for deep breathing. Before you head off in the morning, make your bed and tidy up in a way that says to your future self, "Welcome Home."

5. *Utilize Variable Furniture and Props:* Variable furniture and props maximize the usefulness of your space, especially if you have a smaller home. Things that have multiple uses or are easily broken down and moved to storage will make your space more flexible. This helps a small space seem bigger. Collapsible tables and chairs, bolsters, blankets, and blocks provide more possibilities than typical furniture and create a flow to your home that makes it a more enjoyable place to live.

Variable Furniture and Props

Items that serve multiple purposes allow you to transform your space from host-worthy to child-safe in minutes. Keeping more dynamic belongings allows more customization, variation, and free-dom within your space to meet your evolving needs. Best of all, these items make cleaning and organizing a breeze.

The trapping of conventional furniture and household items is that they are generally permanent fixtures that dominate the rooms they occupy, robbing your home or workspace of spaciousness. By making your furniture semipermanent and your belongings multi-faceted, you restore the space you need to move freely. For instance, if you fold up the leaves of your table and put away your sitting pil-lows before going to bed, there will be more room for your morning movements. It will be easier to pack for work and locate the things you need for your day aided by the flow of your well-organized space. When you return home to the spaciousness you created for yourself, it will be a snap to once again lift the leaves of the table, pass out the sitting pillows, and have friends over for dinner.

The folding table is one of the most useful pieces of variable furniture, especially if it is collapsible and has leaves that make it variable in size. Most of the time you just need enough space for a

Conventional furniture is stagnant and boring. Keeping variable furniture and household items brings life to your home. They make cleaning, orga-nizing, and creating space less complicated and allow your home to adapt more easily to the ever-changing needs of daily life.

modest meal. Only once in a while do you need enough room for a full Thanksgiving spread. Sometimes your table should be a temporary landing place for keys and the mail, and others it should be a place for your children to spread out their art supplies and be creative. Why keep a giant rigid table in your home that you only use twice a year? With the right folding table, you're ready for any occasion, especially the ones that call for no table at all. Folding chairs are also helpful to have around. They make your otherwise chair-free home welcoming to guests who are not accustomed to sitting on the floor. Some items can act as sitting surfaces while also serving other purposes, like the five B's listed below.

The Five B's: Essential Props for a Healing Space

The following is a list of the items I consider to be the most useful for encouraging the practice of active rest. Replace that old, overstuffed armchair that no one wants to sit in with a stack of bolsters and blankets that spark creative sitting arrangements. Reinvent the dining room that no one ever eats in by turning it into your own private self-care studio. Use these items to enrich your practice of active rest throughout the day and to create a nest for sleep-inducing passive rest postures at night. Experiment with each item, and see if you too find them useful. Replace them with items you like more if you don't. Keep looking every day for the things that bring you joy with their usefulness. Keep in mind, it isn't the items themselves but rather the user who makes them useful.

1. **The Bolster**—The bolster (also sometimes called a sitting cushion) is an excellent tool for supporting active rest. Whether you're sitting, kneeling, squatting, or in sphinx pose, there are many ways bolsters can be used to support you. Having lots of bolsters instead of a couch is like being in a room full of pillows where everyone is invited to make themselves comfortable in their own way.

2. **The Blanket**—The blanket is the most variable item on this list because it can take on various shapes. It can become a bolster, a pillow, a mat, or a seat. A strategically placed blanket can be used to support both the knees and ankles

when kneeling. Blankets can be rolled into tubes to be placed under your neck or behind your knees when lying down on the ground. Use blankets to pad bone-to-muscle contact in active rest shapes or as anti-fatigue surfaces to stand and stretch on.

3. **The Block**—Blocks can make postures that are out of reach more doable. Rectangular blocks are particularly helpful as they offer three different heights and varying levels of

Five household items that make your space dynamic and support the practice of active rest are blocks, bolsters, blankets, balls and the bar. Use blocks for making gentle shapes more intense or difficult postures more available. Bolster your hips to make sitting and kneeling sustainable for longer periods of time. Blankets transform easily from something to warm up with to padding for softening bone-to-bone or bone-to-ground contact. Large stability balls replace chairs and make a wide array of exercises available, while small balls are great for self-massage. An overhead bar makes the hanging posture available and can be a place to attach other self-care and exercise equipment.

stability. Use a block to make the ground closer to your hands in squat, or place one below your seat to take some weight off your heels. Still not quite right? Stack another block on top for more lift. Use a block to elevate your hips while sitting, or lie down on one to create a restorative backbend. Blocks can even be useful for deepening postures that you no longer feel a stretch in, like standing on blocks in a forward fold to be able to reach further down. Blocks can also be used to create a standing desk or a desk that allows you to assume other active rest postures.

4. **The Ball**—Balls are playful and teach us a lot about nature and physics. Keep many balls of various shapes, sizes, and textures to offer endless possibilities of expansion to your self-care practice. A tennis ball for massaging the tender muscles between your shoulder blades. A lacrosse ball for massaging the hard fascia on the soles of your feet. A stability ball for stretching your back or replacing your chair. Squeeze a squishy ball rhythmically to release stress and strengthen your grip. Toss a ball to teach a child (or yourself) hand-eye coordination through play or to simply pass the time. Release a whole bag of balls into a spacious room with your children or pets for a guaranteed laugh!

5. **The Bar**–An overhead bar adds a fourth dimension to any room. Just like balls and blocks, the bar is inherently playful. It can quickly change our perspective by allowing us the opportunity to reverse the effects of gravity on our body. Of course, bars make the hanging posture available, but they are also useful for hanging other items overhead. Resistance bands, gymnastics rings, and suspension trainers hung from a bar make more stretching and strengthening exercises possible. A hammock or yoga swing attached to the bar facilitates inversions and other calming shapes.

Recently I invited some clients over for dinner. One attendee was an older woman who originally came to me for weight loss and personal training. She had done some hanging practice with me, so when she saw the gymnastics rings mounted overhead in my living room, she couldn't help showing off her newfound confidence.

Without warning she leapt up, grabbed the rings, and swung back and forth like a kid on monkey bars. "I haven't done that since I was a little girl!" she told the group with an exasperated smile. That night, she was the life of the party, and so too were the rings. Together they inspired playful acrobatics and self-care moments throughout the remainder of the night.

16

Children Are
the World's Greatest
Yoga Teachers

"While we try to teach our children all about life, our children teach us what life is all about."
—Angela Schwindt

I was inspired to write this book by the idea that some indigenous cultures do not suffer chronic pain like we do. I connected this newfound knowledge with the fact that children demonstrate ideal kinesthetics without being trained to do so. I realized that my yoga practice felt so healing because it reconnected me with a lost sense of my youth, a part of myself that had been buried under years of tension and trauma. From there, I theorized that the shapes many of us label "yoga postures" are in fact *innate human postures*, shapes pre-programmed into our DNA that have the power to heal us. I realized that if we hope to have youthful bodies, we must reestablish a connection with our inner child.

This idea fascinated me because it meant I could help my clients heal simply by guiding them to rediscover themselves. It is a core teaching in yoga therapy that the client holds the power to self-heal. The therapist is merely a vector for reconnecting to that power. This power is sometimes referred to as our "inner truth," "center," or "spirit." But phrases like these are often perceived as ethereal, flowery, and even whimsical to many people. The use of labels such as these has the tendency to undermine the work, as they do not direct the practitioner anywhere concrete. Yet the idea that our current problems take root in what our former selves have suffered through is more universally accepted. It is an idea that is the basis for many styles of modern psychotherapy. For clients who do not connect to the notion of an eternal spirit within them, the offering that they seek out a connection with their inner child often lands better and has a greater impact on their practice.

I began to theorize that physical healing also depends on reconnecting with our inner child. Although there is extensive research supporting mental/emotional healing modalities that incorporate inner child work, no one is talking about how this practice can empower physical healing.

I found a small amount of research on the effects of teaching yoga to children, but I have always found this idea odd. Children already do yoga postures and breath practices instinctively, so what is the point of teaching them yoga? There are many children's books available that attempt to teach yoga to kids by encouraging them to stretch like a cat or stand grounded like a tree. But there doesn't seem to be any reference to how children do "yoga" before they are taught, how to encourage the healthy instincts they display naturally, or how to revitalize these behaviors in adults. I had nothing to substantiate my idea.

Then a colossal shift occurred. I found out I was going to be a father! Upon hearing the news I felt fully connected to the sense of youth I was just beginning to rediscover through yoga. Thinking about this mini version of me made me feel alive in a way that I never had before. I gained a new perspective on life. So obvious were all the things that truly mattered, and everything else began to fade away. Before she was even born, Joy was the best yoga teacher I ever had.

Our First Sun Salutation

Fast forward nine months, two weeks, and an arduous five-day labor process, and Joy was finally here. She looked more like an animal than a human, as all newborns do. She displayed only instincts, as her personality was yet to form. I was so excited to see her prove my theory! But at first, she wasn't much of a mover. For the first few months, Joy spent most of her time practicing breathing, eating, and resting deeply.

Then one day, a spark! She reached up and grabbed her toes to demonstrate "happy baby pose." For the next few weeks, she was fascinated with grabbing her feet. She loved to stretch her legs, and if we helped her stretch, she found it hilarious. Of course her pliable body didn't need much help. Instead she seemed to be using the grip of her toes to play a sort of tug-of-war between the muscles of her legs and those of her arms. It was at this point that Joy started demonstrating her ability to quickly build strength and body awareness.

Driven by instinct, Joy began a daily workout routine. Whenever she had the energy, she worked on lifting her head, arms, and legs from a supine position (lying face up). She soon learned that all of this was much easier when she tucked her tail, something she discovered while reaching for her toes. She was performing her first pelvic tilts! I was in awe. Joy was validating everything I had theorized about our playful self-care instincts. She just wanted to explore, to see what she was capable of, and to become more capable each day. When I moved my classes online due to the pandemic, I noticed that Joy was mesmerized by my movements. She loved to watch people move their bodies and try on what she was seeing.

The practice of lifting her bodyweight while supine soon turned into attempts at rolling over. We couldn't resist encouraging her and sometimes even assisting in her many failed attempts at landing prone (face down). After lots of daily strengthening and confidence building, success! She was able to roll over onto her belly. Even though she could only roll over on one side and would then be stuck face down, it became her new favorite thing to do. When she would get tired of being on her belly and frustrated by her attempts to revert, we would pick her up or roll her over. Quickly it became clear that this method of retreat was not satisfying to her. She got upset if we helped her too soon. She wanted to do it herself.

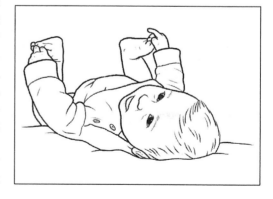

Infants make a gym out of their bodies by grabbing their feet in "happy baby pose." This shape helps them develop dexterity, strength, and a sense of self-control.

16. Children Are the World's Greatest Yoga Teachers

So began a new daily exercise routine. Joy would start her day with some breathing, singing, and crying to let us know she was awake. After a pre-workout snack, she would do some limb lifts and work on rolling over. In the prone position she developed a set of exercises that strengthened her back, arms, and legs. At first, she could only repeat exercises similar to the lifts she was doing from supine. She'd lift her head, arms and legs in different orientations, postures commonly referred to as "locust pose" in yoga. Once lifted she'd try to get her limbs underneath her to find some leverage. Eventually she managed to wedge her arms under her a bit. Voilà! Sphinx pose! This was a huge breakthrough because it made the prone position a place she could hang out in much longer.

Holding sphinx pose was Joy's foundation for building upper body strength. Once her arms were strong enough she started pushing them straight to achieve "cobra pose." Realizing this new capability she began doing lots of baby push-ups. She did yogi style push-ups with hips on the floor, allowing her back to extend as her arms did. A few times she demonstrated an amazing spread out variation of plank pose that many adults would struggle to replicate. All of these new moves led to her ability to flip from prone to supine by doing a push-up, then tucking one arm under and rolling over.

Now my baby was in business. Although she would sometimes get stuck in a position and not know how to get out, she was pleased as a peach to be playing with so many new shapes. Yet she still wasn't satisfied. She wanted desperately to find a position that was more useful than supine and less tiring than prone. She wanted to sit up.

Child development specialists caution parents not to prop infants up in a seat too often, as it slows core muscle development and postural awareness. Knowing this we opted instead to sit her up without back support and to spot her in case of falls. With foundational core, arm, and leg strength in tow from her previous exercise programs, Joy began sitting up on her own. She used her arms to help support her still shaky postural muscles and experimented with many different shapes of her legs, seeking a stronger foundation for sitting. At first she only had the stamina for sitting for a few moments, but eventually these moments grew into minutes.

Achieving sphinx pose is an important developmental milestone because it allows the child to safely be face down. Variations of sphinx are important for developing upper body strength and a sense of independence.

Joy's experiments with the seated and prone positions led to many transitions back and forth over her folded legs as she instinctively practiced posture cycling. She discovered the kneeling position and other sitting orientations this way. A movement pattern was starting to take shape. From her back she would roll over to prone, do a push-up and then shift her hips back into "child's pose" (a kneeling position with arms outstretched). From there she would continue pushing back through a semi-squat into her seat. Eventually she gained enough agency to reverse the pattern and return to her belly.

One day Joy discovered that if she arranged her legs in a butterfly shape while seated and leaned forward she could bounce up and down like she was on a pogo stick. Her new favorite exercise then became bouncing. When she wasn't bouncing up and down in her seat, she was bouncing from a kneeling position. She absolutely loved it, and it was so much fun to watch! My partner and I couldn't resist doing it with her (the kneeling version; we tried the other and determined it was a baby-only move!). It became a morning warm-up routine to wake up our hips and knees. The bouncy dance set a joyful tone for the day. More than just fun, it was a powerful workout that was strengthening Joy's legs, hips and core.

Joy's personality really began to surface. She became more expressive of her needs and wants. She'd reach out to play with things or grab onto surfaces to support herself. She'd motion to us or make sounds to indicate that she wanted a certain book or toy. We always obliged, but again, it was obvious that what she really wanted was to do things for herself. She wanted the ability to go after the things she saw. She began experimenting with ways of getting her legs under her to stand up. Sometimes this meant hanging out inverted in a forward fold for a few moments with her head and hands on the

Once a child can sit up on their own, the world is their oyster. Shifting side to side to arrange their legs in different shapes during play encourages the development of postural muscles. This also improves balance and refines motor control which will be instrumental when learning to walk.

ground. She'd linger there as if she was contemplating the new sensations created by being upside down. It looked like an extreme version of "downward-facing-dog." But it didn't get her anywhere. As the saying goes, she had to crawl before she could walk.

After a few weeks of her bouncing program, Joy worked up the strength, control and confidence to begin

Experimenting with "downward-facing-dog" allows babies to experience a version of standing. This shape is most children's first experience with a self-induced inversion effect and becomes a place they return to for stimulating strong sensory input.

201

trying to crawl. She was slow at first because she couldn't figure out how to alternate her arm and leg movements. After a few weeks of stumbling around, falling, and pushing herself back up, she got it! It was heartwarming to see how happy she was to travel on her own. One day as I was cooking, she suddenly appeared underfoot and put her hand on my leg to say hello. I was so surprised at my child's new ability that I just about broke down in tears.

Now that she had learned to alternate her support from one limb to another, her instincts to reach up and grab things grew stronger. Soon

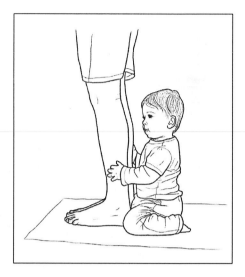

Kneeling is the basis for a child's first experience with locomotion: crawling. The movement patterns created by the combination of standing on the knees and crawling act as simulations for future attempts at standing and walking.

she was pulling herself up into a supported standing position and hanging off the support. Standing and hanging led to "cruising," holding onto supports while sidestepping. It was clear that she was going to start walking soon, yet her foundation wasn't quite complete. There was one more shape she needed to master before learning to walk.

When attempting to stand, children grab onto overhead items and begin practicing hanging. Once they're comfortable with this, they begin "cruising," walking while hanging onto something. This makes hanging an important milestone on the journey to walking.

To walk unsupported Joy needed more strength and control in her hips. Instinctively she knew that squatting was the most effective exercise for this. It was the missing link from the ground positions she had mastered to the new challenge of standing and walking. She naturally landed in the squat shape while experimenting with various movement patterns. From a kneeling position she pushed back into her semi-squat, then attempted to erect her spine while keeping her hands on the ground. After getting her legs underneath her, she'd hang or cruise for a bit, then slowly squat down to a seat for a rest. Once she was accustomed to it, Joy utilized the squat more than any other position. Over the next few months, she performed hundreds of squats in many different variations. Through the squat, all her capabilities soared.

Watching Joy's journey towards walking was like witnessing the development of *our first sun salutation*. A sun salutation is a sequence of yoga postures that join together to create a mindful movement pattern united with the breath. Different yoga lineages have different sun salutations. These movement patterns utilize the kinesthetic capabilities of our body to develop strength, flexibility, and control. They are foundational practices that are often seen as prerequisites to performing more intense postures.

From observing Joy's playmates I realized that our first sun salutation is a unique movement pattern individualized by

The squat position leverages the large muscles of the lower body well, creating a stable base. Once they discover the squat and hanging positions, children assist themselves from squat to standing, then back into squat many times throughout the day. This builds the strength and coordination necessary for walking.

the child performing it. Factors like genetics, nurturing, and modeling are likely to affect the way this progression arises. Joy's variation seemed so natural and ergonomic once she had mastered all the pieces. From her back she would roll over onto her belly. Then she would push up into sphinx, then back into a kneeling position. Next, she would push back to a seat or squat, then perform a full depth squat (sometimes aided by hanging) in order to stand all the way up. It was remarkable how fast she demonstrated all the postures in this book.

In fact, at the early age of nine months old, Joy took her first steps. It wasn't as grand of a moment as I was expecting. In fact, it was pretty anticlimactic. That long walk across the room from one parent to the other we see in movies is totally unrealistic. Just like all the other movements she had mastered previously, it started as one or two "maybe" steps which she repeated for a few weeks before we could confidently say she was walking. There was even a period of time when only one foot would do the stepping, which is when Joy discovered her love for spinning. At first it seemed like meaningless fun, but each bout of spinning became more and more controlled. This innate movement gradually trained her vestibular system, improving her balance and coordination.

Although her first steps weren't remarkable, watching the journey of Joy learn and finally demonstrate her first sun salutation was amazing.

Learning to walk is a milestone for children no parent will forget. Yet we so easily forget the journey it took to get there and the basic human shapes that paved the way. If we encourage their freedom, we see that children continue utilize these shapes for work, play and rest well into young adulthood. If we return to this practice, our bodies will become supple, resilient, and capable like theirs once again.

She demonstrated that not only are these postures innate, but they are essential to building and maintaining the capabilities of our bodies. After mastering the eight essential healing postures, Joy went on a mission to spread the word of self-healing through her playful exuberance. Wherever she went she had the power to diffuse tension and make everyone around her smile. She didn't care much for seats, and if she was strapped to one for too long, it was sure to become a jungle gym. When graced with her presence, people would immediately mimic her. They would take a big breath, gasp-

There's a reason children don't sit still for long. It hurts! The more we keep our bodies moving and assume healthy shapes, the less we suffer from pain and disease and the more joyful our lives become.

ing with delight. Their voices would change. Their faces would light up and their posture would follow suit. If they weren't trapped by a badly broken body or mind, they would squat, kneel, or sit on the ground to greet her at eye level. Joy was teaching yoga to everyone around her, whether they knew it or not.

Why We Hurt

The postures and practices offered in this book are not owned by indigenous people. They are not owned by the yogis or the Japanese. These are *human* practices. They are your birthright. Whether you can remember them or not, you have performed all of these practices before. You were once a master of your body. You don't need to pretend that you are an indigenous person or become a yogi to be capable of pain-free existence. Rather, you need to rediscover yourself. You need to rediscover who you really are at your core. You need to reconnect with a part of you that has always been there, tugging at your pant leg and saying, "Ooh ooh, I have the answer! Pick me, pick me!"

When you were a child, you had superpowers—superpowers like rapidly growing intellect, perpetual presence within the moment, and the ability to spontaneously self-heal. Your instincts encouraged you to learn as much as possible every day. You amazed everyone around you with your ability to quickly grasp new concepts, to understand language, solve problems, and utilize tools in a way no other young creature on the planet can. Your instincts encouraged you to remain aware of yourself and everything around you. You never thought of anything else than the present moment. You lived in a state adults might refer to as bliss, nirvana, or heaven on earth. You were not regretful of the past nor were you anxious about the future. You just were, right then and there, exploring your body and your environment. Just living life.

Your instincts encouraged you to push yourself and those around you to the edge of your comfort zone every day, always eager to discover what you were physically capable of. Pushing like this made your body grow so fast that it was often painful. When you experienced pain, you instinctively leaned on others, sought out rest and other healthy ways to cope. Soon you were capable of movements and postures that the adults around you might never attempt again. They marveled at your abilities, having forgotten that they were once just like you. Your capabilities grew so quickly that you couldn't be trusted by yourself. It was too easy to get into something you shouldn't, break something important, or hurt yourself or the cat. Most wonderful of all you were so focused on the present moment, your mind so malleable and your body so resilient, that you forgot your mistakes and pain quickly. You were able to self-heal rapidly simply by resting.

These instincts still exist within you. If you are chronically sick or in pain, you can relieve what ails you by reconnecting with them.

Something is standing in the way of your accessing your self-healing capabilities. Maybe it's the trappings of modern life, or maybe it's your busy mind. It's likely healthy instincts still pop up in the background once in a while when you are in pain or stressed, but you don't act upon them because you've forgotten how. Sometime during childhood or young adulthood these instincts were buried under social and environmental conditioning. The healthy coping mechanisms you once created were replaced by unhealthy habits. Following this path, our traumas are never dealt with. This is why we hurt.

If you look back far enough, you might remember the moments that threw the first few fistfuls of dirt on top of your self-healing instincts. They might have been as benign as cruel comments from other kids. Or they may have been traumatizing moments of abuse that hurt you so deeply it caused you to cave in on yourself for protection.

Most likely, it was lots of little things. The seats you were stuffed into and told not to move from for hours on end. The screens that stole your attention away from your body. The sacrifices you made to fit into a culture that doesn't value well-being as highly as it does social status. The clothes you thought were cool, the places you thought were fun, and the people you thought you wanted to be like. Your thoughts began to overtake your instincts. Soon your thinking mind took over how you showed up in the world. You created a disguise that you could wear in public to protect yourself from harm. You became your ego, and the first thing to suffer was your body.

Reconnecting with Your Inner Child

When adults are stuck in aching bodies and toxic thought patterns, oftentimes the solution to their problems is simple: to reconnect with their inner child. Each of us has a little one hidden deep inside, yearning to be seen and longing to be embraced. The child inside us contains the instincts we've lost that we need for self-healing. If we look to children who have not yet experienced trauma, we see the mental and physical freedom missing from adulthood.

When raised in spacious freedom, children aren't afraid to act natural: to lie down in the dirt, to squat down and inspect a bug, or to jump into a puddle to feel what it's like to make a splash. When we reconnect with our inner child, a sense of relief fills our body. Relieved from the burdens of being an adult we relax deeply. In this relaxed state we heal spontaneously. We return to our true selves.

Reconnecting with your inner child will be a great challenge. Perhaps the greatest challenge you have faced as an adult. It will be uncomfortable, sometimes even painful. It may feel quite tragic to touch upon the innocence you've lost. It will stir up emotions and memories you buried long ago. This therapeutic discomfort is an inextricable part of the healing process. Just as we feel physical discomfort when we are stretching a previously injured part of the body, so too do we experience mental and spiritual discomfort when we reconnect with our true selves. However, if you resolve to revisit this connection whenever you feel lost, the rewards will be immense—rewards such as a pain-free body, a peaceful mind, and a deep connection to all the wonders of life available in the present moment.

When attempting to reconnect with your inner child, I recommend not going it alone. Most of us will need guides who know the path and what the journey is like: Friends, family, teachers, or professionals who you trust are an imperative part of safely rediscovering yourself. Look for people who have been on a healing journey themselves, people you trust to keep you safe through the power of their empathy. The parts of you that need your attention in order to heal will reveal themselves alongside the original sources of your pain. A strong guide is someone who can help you discern friend or foe when walking the path to healing, so you can stay connected with your true self and let go of the things that no longer serve you.

Spending Time with Children— The World's Greatest Yoga Class

How do we go about reconnecting with our inner child? Three simple ways to reconnect with your inner child are to explore nature, explore the body, and of course, spend time with children. Nature brings us back to our primal sense of self, which is synonymous with our inner child. Here I will describe what it's like to explore the body while guided by our inner child and how this practice is amplified by spending time with children.

In order to explore our body like a child, we need to be willing to play like a child. I don't mean running around the house like an unruly toddler, screaming at the top of your lungs (although that does sound like it would feel kind of good right now...). It's not the exact actions that children perform which make play therapeutic. Rather it's the mindset of the child and their ability to rely on instincts for guidance that make children the world's greatest yoga teachers. There are instances where joining children in their method of play is safe and immediately activates our self-healing capabilities. Activities like swinging with a child, reading them a silly picture book, or building a sandcastle with them will be healing for both of you. However, sometimes the type of play that is stimulating and safe for a child's body and mind might not be appropriate for you right now. The type of play that will benefit you the most is probably some kind of therapeutic exercise like those mentioned in Part One.

For you, play might mean behaving in ways you haven't in many years. It might mean experimenting with new movements or sensations you've been too busy to explore. Play in your body could be as simple as a minute of active rest in one of the eight essential healing postures. It could be walking barefoot on surfaces you haven't touched since you were a child just to remember what it feels like. Play for you may be staring up at the sky and opening your mouth to taste the rain or lying down on the ground to smell the earth. When you follow the instincts of your inner child, play will show up naturally in your life.

The challenge in starting this practice is knowing the difference between your habits and your instincts. They can feel very similar. You may have developed the habit of bending over to pick things up with a curved spine and a tucked tail, a position that puts your body in danger. This is not the same as the instinct we have as children to get closer to the object by bending down into a squat. The next time you bend over to pick something up, listen more closely to your body. It will tell you that your old habits are hurting it. Your body will tell you to engage and move mindfully. Your body has the answers. You must learn to listen to your body once again, like you did when you were a child.

The best way to rediscover your instincts is to witness them in others. If you have the opportunity to do so, spend more time with the children in your life. Observe them closely. Notice how they are more likely to rely on the structure of their body for supporting actions rather than artificial support. See how they take pleasure in simple things, like the sensations produced by movement or the beauty of something ordinary. Witness how they instinctively gravitate towards nature for entertainment when there's no screen sucking them inside.

Most importantly, notice how they focus with intention on what they are doing instead of thinking about when they fell down a few minutes ago or what game they are going to play next. This practice frees the mind and soothes the body. Very aware of themselves, children respond to the needs of the body quickly, effortlessly practicing biofeedback in each passing moment, keeping discomfort from growing into bigger problems.

Every parent has experienced the following scenario. Their little one is giving subtle cues that

When we lie down, we are revisiting a shape that activates an ancient part of us. Barely understood functions like sleep proven to be essential for healthy human life are optimized by this shape. Curled up in the fetal position we return to the shape of a human embryo, the original shape of our body which coincides with the most rapid stage of growth in our entire existence. Lying down and spreading our body out on the Earth, we reconnect with our first attempts to fight off the fragility of the human form, expressing the instincts encoded in us that have enabled human beings to thrive for thousands of years.

210

something is wrong: tugging at their clothes, pointing at their body, and whimpering that leads to whining. While we absentmindedly search for a solution, crying progresses into full meltdown mode. When we finally discover what the problem is, we realize how simple the fix is. Their onesie was on too tight. They were hungry. They had a full diaper. Most problems have simple remedies, ones that are obvious and easy to discover if we slow down and look deeply into the present moment.

This is the story of our bodies. We are the children asking for attention. Our broken backs are the products of not giving ourselves the daily attention we need. Our battered bodies are like a baby's bottom that hasn't been changed soon enough. At first it was a slight discomfort that needed only a gentle shift to be alleviated. Sitting in discomfort too long, it grew painful. Then it made us sick. Repeated over the course of decades, it deformed us and robbed us of the ability to access the joy available all around us.

Pay attention to your body from now on. It will tell you what it needs. If you've forgotten how to pay attention, just take a deep breath. Step outside. Leave behind the things you do not truly need for survival. Spend time with children. Remember yourself as a child. Take time to identify what's standing in your way. All the answers lie within you. You just need to wake up and listen.

Chapter Notes

Chapter 1

1. Hewes, Gordon W. "The Anthropology of Posture." *Scientific American*, 1957. https://www.scientificamerican.com/article/the-anthropology-of-posture/.

2. Olshansky, S. Jay, et al. "A Potential Decline in Life Expectancy in the United States in the 21st Century: NEJM." *New England Journal of Medicine*, March 17, 2005. https://www.nejm.org/doi/full/10.1056/NEJMsr043743#t=article.

3. Morris, J.N., J.A. Heady, P.A.B. Raffle, et al. "Coronary Heart Disease and Physical Activity of Work." *Lancet*, 1953. https://www.sciencedirect.com/science/article/abs/pii/S0140673653914950.

4. "Physical Activity." World Health Organization. November 26, 2020. https://www.who.int/news-room/fact-sheets/detail/physical-activity.

5. Patel, Alpa V., Leslie Bernstein, Anusila Deka, Heather Spencer Feigelson, Peter T. Campbell, Susan M. Gapstur, Graham A. Colditz, and Michael J. Thun. "Leisure Time Spent Sitting in Relation to Total Mortality in a Prospective Cohort of U.S. Adults." OUP Academic. Oxford University Press, July 22, 2010. https://academic.oup.com/aje/article/172/4/419/85345#639953.

6. "Sedentary Behavior Increases the Risk of Certain Cancers." OUP Academic. Oxford University Press, June 14, 2014. https://academic.oup.com/jnci/article/106/7/dju206/1010488.

7. Howard, Jacqueline. "The U.S. Suicide Rate Is up 33% since 1999, Research Says." CNN, June 21, 2019. https://www.cnn.com/2019/06/20/health/suicide-rates-nchs-study/index.html.

8. Raichlen, David A., Herman Pontzer, Theodore W. Zderic, Jacob A. Harris, Audax Z. P. Mabulla, Marc T. Hamilton, and Brian M. Wood. "Sitting, Squatting, and the Evolutionary Biology of Human Inactivity." PNAS. National Academy of Sciences, March 31, 2020. https://www.pnas.org/content/117/13/7115.

9. Searing, Linda. "The Big Number: The Average U.S. Adult Sits 6.5 Hours a Day. For Teens, It's Even More." *The Washington Post*. WP Company, April 28, 2019. https://www.washingtonpost.com/national/health-science/the-big-numberthe-average-us-adult-sits-65-hours-a-day-for-teens-its-even-more/2019/04/26/7c29e4c2–676a-11e9-a1b6-b29b90efa879_story.html.

Chapter 2

1. Gokhale, Esther, and Susan Adams. *8 Steps to a Pain-Free Back: Natural Posture Solutions for Pain in the Back, Neck, Shoulder, Hip, Knee, and Foot.* Chichester: Lotus Publishing, 2013.

2. Barone, Francine. "A Cross-Cultural Look at Posture in EHRAF." Human Relations Area Files—Cultural information for education and research, May 20, 2016. https://hraf.yale.edu/a-cross-cultural-look-at-posture-in-ehraf/.

Chapter Notes

Chapter 3

1. Zautra, Alex J., Robert Fasman, Mary C. Davis, and Arthur D. (Bud) Craig. "The Effects of Slow Breathing on Affective Responses to Pain Stimuli: An Experimental Study." *PAIN®*. No longer published by Elsevier, January 15, 2010. https://www.sciencedirect.com/science/article/abs/pii/S0304395909005740.

2. Omidi, Abdollah, and Fatemeh Zargar. "Effect of Mindfulness-Based Stress Reduction on Pain Severity and Mindful Awareness in Patients with Tension Headache: A Randomized Controlled Clinical Trial." Nursing and midwifery studies. Kashan University of Medical Sciences, September 2014. https://www.ncbi.nlm.nih.gov/pmc/articles/PMC4332994/.

3. Grant, Joshua, and Pierre Rainville. "Pain Sensitivity and Analgesic Effects of Mindful States in Zen Meditators: A Cross-Sectional Study." LWW. *Psychosomatic Medicine*, January 2009. https://journals.lww.com/psychosomaticmedicine/Abstract/2009/01000/Pain_Sensitivity_and_Analgesic_Effects_of_Mindful.17.aspx.

Chapter 4

1. Sarno, John E. *Mind Over Back Pain: A Radically New Approach to the Diagnosis and Treatment of Back Pain*. New York: Berkley Books, 1999.

2. Coles, Nicholas A., Jeff T. Larsen, and Heather C. Lench. "A meta-analysis of the facial feedback literature: Effects of facial feedback on emotional experience are small and variable." *Psychological Bulletin*, 2019. Originally found at https://www.sciencedaily.com/releases/2019/04/190412094728.htm.

3. Cuddy, Amy, Jack Schultz, and Nathan Fosse. "P-Curving a More Comprehensive Body of Research on Postural Feedback Reveals Clear Evidential Value for Power-Posing Effects: Reply to Simmons and Simonsohn." SAGE Journals, March 2018. https://journals.sagepub.com/eprint/CzbNAn7Ch6ZZirK9yMGH/full.

Chapter 5

1. Buckthorpe, Matthew, Matthew Stride, and Francesco Della Villa. "Assessing and Treating Gluteus Maximus Weakness—A Clinical Commentary." International Journal of Sports Physical Therapy. Sports Physical Therapy Section, July 2019. https://www.ncbi.nlm.nih.gov/pmc/articles/PMC6670060/.

2. Noro, Kageyu, Rani Lueder, Shunji Yamada, Goroh Fujimaki, Hideki Oyama, and Yuki Hashidate. "Revisiting Sitting Cross-Cultural Aspects of Seating." SAGE Journals, 2006. https://journals.sagepub.com/doi/abs/10.1177/154193120605000704?journalCode=proe.

3. Peper, Erik, Richard Harvey, Lauren Mason, and I-Mei Lin. "Do Better in Math: How Your Body Posture May Change Stereotype Threat Response." *NeuroRegulation*, 2018. http://www.neuroregulation.org/article/view/18396.

4. Brito, L.B., D.R. Ricardo, D.S. Araújo, P.S. Ramos, J. Myers, and C.G. Araújo. "Ability to Sit and Rise from the Floor as a Predictor of All-Cause Mortality." *European Journal of Preventive Cardiology*. U.S. National Library of Medicine, 2012. https://pubmed.ncbi.nlm.nih.gov/23242910/.

Chapter 7

1. Dekker, Rebecca. "Evidence on: Birthing Positions." Evidence Based Birth," June 29, 2020. https://evidencebasedbirth.com/evidence-birthing-positions/.

2. Donovan, Francesca. "This Is How Much of Your Life You've Spent on the Toilet." *Unilad*, April 2018. https://www.unilad.co.uk/featured/this-is-how-much-of-your-life-youve-spent-on-the-toilet/.

Chapter 8

1. Dov, Sikirov. "Comparison of Straining during Defecation in Three Positions: Results and Implications for Human Health." *Digestive Diseases and Sciences*. U.S. National Library of Medicine,

2003. https://pubmed.ncbi.nlm.nih. gov/12870773/.

2. Ahmed, Imtiaz, et al. "Role of Defecation Postures on the Outcome of Chronic Anal Fissure." *Pakistan Journal of Surgery*, 2013. http://www.pjs.com.pk/ journal_pdfs/oct-dec13/269.pdf.

3. Golay, Jane, Saraswathi Vedam, and Leo Sorger. "The Squatting Position for the Second Stage of Labor: Effects on Labor and on Maternal and Fetal Well-Being." Wiley Online Library. John Wiley & Sons, Ltd., April 2, 2007. https:// onlinelibrary.wiley.com/doi/abs/10.1111/ j.1523–536X.1993.tb00420.x.

4. Dekker, Rebecca. "Evidence on: Birthing Positions." Evidence Based Birth," June 29, 2020. https://evidencebasedbirth. com/evidence-birthing-positions/.

5. Dekker, Rebecca. "Evidence on: Birthing Positions." Evidence Based Birth," June 29, 2020. https://evidencebasedbirth. com/evidence-birthing-positions/.

Chapter 9

1. Shuval, Kerem, et al. "Standing, Obesity, and Metabolic Syndrome." Mayo Clinic, 2015. https://www.mayo clinicproceedings.org/article/S0025- 6196(15)00628-X/abstract.

2. Creasy, S.A., R.J. Rogers, T.D. Byard, R.J. Kowalsky, and J.M. Jakicic. "Energy Expenditure During Acute Periods of Sitting, Standing, and Walking." *Journal of Physical Activity & Health*. U.S. National Library of Medicine, December 2015. https://pubmed.ncbi.nlm.nih. gov/26693809/.

3. Healy, Genevieve N., et al. "Replacing sitting by standing or stepping: associations with cardio-metabolic risk biomarkers." *European Heart Journal*, July 2015. Originally accessed at https://www.sciencedaily. com/releases/2015/07/150730220021.htm.

4. Henson, Joseph, Melanie J. Davies, Danielle H. Bodicoat, Charlotte L. Edwardson, Jason M.R. Gill, David J. Stensel, Keith Tolfrey, David W. Dunstan, Kamlesh Khunti, and Thomas Yates. "Breaking Up Prolonged Sitting With Standing or Walking Attenuates the Postprandial Metabolic Response in Postmenopausal Women: A Randomized Acute Study." *Diabetes Care.* American Diabetes Association, November 30, 2015. https://care.diabetesjournals.org/ content/early/2015/11/29/dc15–1240.

5. Rettner, Rachael. "Prolonged Sitting Linked to Breast and Colon Cancers." *LiveScience*. Purch, May 30, 2013. https://www. livescience.com/35953-prolonged-sitting-raises-breast-colon-cancer-risk.html.

6. Wilmot E.G., C.L. Edwardson, F.A. Achana, M.J. Davies, T. Gorely, L.J. Gray, K. Khunti, T. Yates, and S.J. Biddle. "Sedentary time in adults and the association with diabetes, cardiovascular disease and death: systematic review and meta-analysis." *Diabetologia*. 2012. https://pubmed.ncbi.nlm. nih.gov/22890825/.

7. Katzmarzyk P.T., and I.M. Lee. "Sedentary behaviour and life expectancy in the USA: a cause-deleted life table analysis." BMJ Open, 2012. https://pubmed. ncbi.nlm.nih.gov/22777603/.

8. Ognibene, Grant T., Wilson Torres, Rie von Eyben, and Kathleen C. Horst. "Impact of a Sit-Stand Workstation on Chronic Low Back Pain." *Journal of Occupational and Environmental Medicine*, March 2016. https://journals.lww.com/ joem/Citation/2016/03000/Impact_of_a_ Sit_Stand_Workstation_on_Chronic_ Low.11.aspx.

9. Pronk, N.P., A.S. Katz, M. Lowry, and J.R. Payfer. "Reducing occupational sitting time and improving worker health: the Take-a-Stand Project." Preventing Chronic Disease. 2011. https://www.ncbi. nlm.nih.gov/pmc/articles/PMC3477898/.

10. Thorp A.A., B.A. Kingwell, N. Owen, and D.W. Dunstan. "Breaking up workplace sitting time with intermittent standing bouts improves fatigue and musculoskeletal discomfort in overweight/ obese office workers." *Occupational and Environmental Medicine*, November 2014. https://pubmed.ncbi.nlm.nih. gov/25168375/.

11. Knight A.P., and M. Baer. "Get Up, Stand Up: The Effects of a Non-Sedentary Workspace on Information Elaboration and Group Performance." *Social, Psychological and Personality Science*, 2014. https://journals.sagepub.com/doi/ abs/10.1177/1948550614538463.

Chapter Notes

12. Garrett, Gregory, et al. "Call Center Productivity Over 6 Months Following a Standing Desk Intervention." Taylor & Francis, December 2015. https://www.tandfonline.com/doi/full/10.1080/21577323.2016.1183534?scroll=top&needAccess=true.

13. DiPietro, Loretta, Andrei Gribok, Michelle S. Stevens, Larry F. Hamm, and William Rumpler. "Three 15-Min Bouts of Moderate Postmeal Walking Significantly Improves 24-h Glycemic Control in Older People at Risk for Impaired Glucose Tolerance." *Diabetes Care.* American Diabetes Association, June 11, 2013. https://care.diabetesjournals.org/content/early/2013/06/03/dc13–0084.

14. Zheng, H., N. Orsini, J. Amin, A. Wolk, V.T. Nguyen, and F. Ehrlich. "Quantifying the dose-response of walking in reducing coronary heart disease risk: meta-analysis." *European Journal of Epidemiology*, 2009. https://pubmed.ncbi.nlm.nih.gov/19306107/

15. Dunlop, Dorothy D., Jing Song, Jennifer M. Hootman, Michael C. Nevitt, Pamela A. Semanik, Jungwha Lee, Leena Sharma, et al. "One Hour a Week: Moving to Prevent Disability in Adults With Lower Extremity Joint Symptoms." *American Journal of Preventive Medicine.* Elsevier, March 20, 2019. https://www.sciencedirect.com/science/article/abs/pii/S0749379719300455.

16. Johansson, Marcus, Terry Hartig, and Henk Staats. "Psychological Benefits of Walking: Moderation by Company and Outdoor Environment." *International Association of Applied Psychology.* John Wiley & Sons, Ltd, August 4, 2011. https://iaap-journals.onlinelibrary.wiley.com/doi/abs/10.1111/j.1758–0854.2011.01051.x.

17. Barton, J., R. Hine, and J. Pretty. "The Health Benefits of Walking in Greenspaces of High Natural and Heritage Value." Taylor & Francis, 2008. https://www.tandfonline.com/doi/full/10.1080/19438150903378425.

18. Roe, Jenny, and Peter Aspinall. "The Restorative Benefits of Walking in Urban and Rural Settings in Adults with Good and Poor Mental Health." *Health & Place.* Pergamon, November 10, 2010. https://www.sciencedirect.com/science/article/abs/pii/S1353829210001322.

19. Lee, I.M., and David Buchner. "The Importance of Walking to Public Health." Medicine and Science in Sports and Exercise. U.S. National Library of Medicine, 2008. https://pubmed.ncbi.nlm.nih.gov/18562968/.

Chapter 10

1. Mitchell, C., A. Adebajo, E. Hay, and A. Carr. "Shoulder pain: diagnosis and management in primary care." *British Medical Journal*, 2005. https://www.ncbi.nlm.nih.gov/pmc/articles/PMC1283277/#:~:text=Self%20reported%20prevalence%20of%20shoulder,with%20new%20shoulder%20pain%20annually.

2. Paavola, Hike, Antti Malmivaara, Simo Taimela, Kari Kanto, Jari Inkinen, Juha Kalske, Ilkka Sinisaari, Vesa Savolainen, Jonas Ranstam, and Teppo L.N. Järvinen. "Subacromial decompression versus diagnostic arthroscopy for shoulder impingement: randomised, placebo surgery controlled clinical trial." *British Medical Journal*, 2018. https://www.sciencedaily.com/releases/2018/07/180720092518.htm.

3. Townsend, Joseph B., and Susan Barton. "The Impact of Ancient Tree Form on Modern Landscape Preferences." Urban Forestry & Urban Greening. Urban & Fischer, June 18, 2018. https://www.sciencedirect.com/science/article/pii/S1618866718301146.

4. Kirsch, John M. *Shoulder Pain? The Solution & Prevention.* Morgan Hill, CA: Bookstand Publishing, 2019.

5. Rantanen T., J.M. Guralnik, D. Foley, et al. "Midlife Hand Grip Strength as a Predictor of Old Age Disability." *Journal of the American Medical Association*, 1999. https://jamanetwork.com/journals/jama/fullarticle/188748.

Chapter 11

1. Braley, Pam. "The Vestibular System." *The Inspired Treehouse*, March 2014. https://theinspiredtreehouse.com/vestibular/.

2. Ashburner, Jill, Laura Bennett, Sylvia Rodger, and Jenny Ziviani. "Understanding the Sensory Experiences of Young People with Autism Spectrum Disorder: A Preliminary Investigation." Wiley Online Library. John Wiley & Sons, Ltd, January 10, 2013. https://onlinelibrary.wiley.com/doi/abs/10.1111/1440–1630.12025.

3. Rine, Rose Marie. "Vestibular Rehabilitation for Children." Seminars in hearing. Thieme Medical Publishers, August 2018. ttps://www.ncbi.nlm.nih.gov/pmc/articles/PMC6054578/.

4. Brownlee, Nancy, Martha Foster, Donald P. Griffith, and C. Eugene Carlton. "Controlled Inversion Therapy: an Adjunct to the Elimination of Gravity-Dependent Fragments Following Extracorporeal Shock Wave Lithotripsy." *The Journal of Urology*, June 1990. https://www.auajournals.org/doi/abs/10.1016/S0022–5347%2817%-2940196–0.

5. Papp, M.E., Lindfors, P., Storck, N., et al. "Increased heart rate variability but no effect on blood pressure from 8 weeks of hatha yoga—a pilot study." BioMed Central, 2013. https://doi.org/10.1186/1756–0500-6-59.

6. Marcelo Campos, M.D. "Heart Rate Variability: A New Way to Track Well-Being." Harvard Health Blog, October 24, 2019. https://www.health.harvard.edu/blog/heart-rate-variability-new-way-track-well-2017112212789.

7. Tyagi A., and M. Cohen. "Yoga and heart rate variability: A comprehensive review of the literature." *International Journal of Yoga*, 2016. https://www.ncbi.nlm.nih.gov/pmc/articles/PMC4959333/.

8. Breit, Sigrid, Aleksandra Kupferberg, Gerhard Rogler, and Gregor Hasler. "Vagus Nerve as Modulator of the Brain–Gut Axis in Psychiatric and Inflammatory Disorders." *Frontiers*, February 1, 2018. https://www.frontiersin.org/articles/10.3389/fpsyt.2018.00044/full?fbclid=IwAR3PA3EFjHZPgy0zsChJWyJMyVGkKyPM7SN7UDb2vCTuOCl97Ob2SQabkRo.

9. Manjunath Prasad, K.S., Barbara A. Gregson, Gerard Hargreaves, Tiernan Byrnes, Philip Winburn, and A. David Mendelow. "Inversion therapy in patients with pure single level lumbar discogenic disease: a pilot randomized trial." *Disability and Rehabilitation*, 2012. https://www.tandfonline.com/doi/abs/10.3109/09638288.2011.647231.

10. Jee, Yong-Seok. "The effect of inversion traction on pain sensation, lumbar flexibility and trunk muscles strength in patients with chronic low back pain." *Isokinetics and Exercise Science*, 2013. https://www.researchgate.net/publication/264742284_The_effect_of_inversion_traction_on_pain_sensation_lumbar_flexibility_and_trunk_muscles_strength_in_patients_with_chronic_low_back_pain.

Chapter 12

1. Mustian, Karen, et al. "Multicenter, randomized controlled trial of yoga for sleep quality among cancer survivors." *Journal of Clinical Oncology*, 2013.

2. Gnanalatha, R.A.H. "A Study on the Effect of Savasana and Suryanamaskara on Blood Pressure." Institute of Indigenous Medicine, 2007. http://192.248.16.117:8080/research/bitstream/70130/2532/1/Dr.R.A.H.Gnanalatha.pdf.

3. Alderman, B., R. Olson, C. Brush, et al. "MAP training: combining meditation and aerobic exercise reduces depression and rumination while enhancing synchronized brain activity." *Translational Psychiatry*, 2016. https://doi.org/10.1038/tp.2015.225.

4. Neethu, M.D. "Effectiveness of Savasana on Blood Pressure Among Patients with Hypertension—A Quasi Experimental Study." *International Journal of Research in Engineering, Science and Management*, 2020. https://www.ijresm.com/Vol.3_2020/Vol3_Iss2_February20/IJRESM_V3_I2_96.pdf.

5. Santaella, Danilo, et al. "Yoga Relaxation (Savasana) Decreases Cardiac Sympathovagal Balance in Hypertensive Patients." *Medical Express*, 2014. https://cdn.publisher.gn1.link/medicalexpress.net.br/pdf/v1n5a04.pdf.

6. Tetley, M. "Instinctive sleeping and resting postures: an anthropological and zoological approach to treatment of low

back and joint pain." *British Medical Journal*, 2000. https://www.ncbi.nlm.nih.gov/pmc/articles/PMC1119282/.

Chapter 13

1. Li, Q., K. Morimoto, A. Nakadai, et al. "Forest Bathing Enhances Human Natural Killer Activity and Expression of Anti-Cancer Proteins." *International Journal of Immunopathology and Pharmacology*, April 2007.

2. Li, Q., K. Morimoto, M. Kobayashi, et al. "Visiting a Forest, but Not a City Increases Human Natural Killer Activity and Expression of Anti-Cancer Proteins." *International Journal of Immunopathology and Pharmacology*, January 2008.

3. Mao, Gen-Xiang, Yong-Bao Cao, Xiao-Guang Lan, Zhi-Hua He, Zhuo-Mei Chen, Ya-Zhen Wang, Xi-Lian Hu, Yuan-Dong Lv, Guo-Fu Wang, and Jing Yan. "Therapeutic Effect of Forest Bathing on Human Hypertension in the Elderly." *Journal of Cardiology*. Elsevier, September 1, 2012. https://www.sciencedirect.com/science/article/pii/S0914508712001852.

4. Bielinis, Ernest, Norimasa Takayama, Sergii Boiko, Aneta Omelan, and Lidia Bielinis. "The Effect of Winter Forest Bathing on Psychological Relaxation of Young Polish Adults." Urban Forestry & Urban Greening. Urban & Fischer, December 16, 2017. https://www.sciencedirect.com/science/article/abs/pii/S1618866717304296.

5. Sinatra, S.T., J.L. Oschman, G. Chevalier, and D. Sinatra. "Electric Nutrition: The Surprising Health and Healing Benefits of Biological Grounding (Earthing)." *Alternative Therapies in Health and Medicine*, 2017. https://pubmed.ncbi.nlm.nih.gov/28987038/.

6. Brown, Dick, Gaétan Chevalier, and Michael Hill. "Pilot Study on the Effect of Grounding on Delayed-Onset Muscle Soreness." Mary Ann Liebert, Inc., Publishers, March 2, 2010. https://www.liebertpub.com/doi/full/10.1089/acm.2009.0399.

7. Müller, Erich, et al. "Effectiveness of Grounded Sleeping on Recovery After Intensive Eccentric Muscle Loading." *Frontiers in Physiology*, January 2019. https://www.ncbi.nlm.nih.gov/pmc/articles/PMC6360250/.

8. Brown, Richard, et al. "Grounding after moderate eccentric contractions reduces muscle damage." Open Access *Journal of Sports Medicine*, September 2015. https://www.ncbi.nlm.nih.gov/pmc/articles/PMC4590684/.

9. Passi, R., K. Doheny, Y. Gordin, H. Hinssen, and C. Palmer. "Electrical Grounding Improves Vagal Tone in Preterm Infants." *Neonatology*, 2017. https://www.karger.com/Article/Abstract/475744#.

10. Ober, Clinton, Stephen T. Sinatra, and Martin Zucker. *Earthing: the Most Important Health Discovery Ever!* Laguna Beach, CA: Basic Health Publications, 2014.

Chapter 15

1. Schmeer, Kammi K., and Aimee J. Yoon. "Home sweet home? Home physical environment and inflammation in children." Social Science Research, 2016. https://www.ncbi.nlm.nih.gov/pmc/articles/PMC5116303/.

2. Lee, Ingrid. "The Joy of Abundance." *Time*—Special Edition: The Power of Joy, 2020.

Bibliography

Ahmed, Imtiaz, et al. "Role of Defecation Postures on the Outcome of Chronic Anal Fissure." *Pakistan Journal of Surgery*, 2013. http://www.pjs.com.pk/journal_pdfs/oct-dec13/269.pdf.

Alderman, B., R. Olson, C. Brush, et al. "MAP training: combining meditation and aerobic exercise reduces depression and rumination while enhancing synchronized brain activity." *Translational Psychiatry*, 2016. https://doi.org/10.1038/tp.2015.225.

Ashburner, Jill, Laura Bennett, Sylvia Rodger, and Jenny Ziviani. "Understanding the Sensory Experiences of Young People with Autism Spectrum Disorder: A Preliminary Investigation." Wiley Online Library. John Wiley & Sons, Ltd, January 10, 2013. https://onlinelibrary.wiley.com/doi/abs/10.1111/1440–1630.12025.

Barone, Francine. "A Cross-Cultural Look at Posture in EHRAF." Human Relations Area Files—Cultural information for education and research, May 20, 2016. https://hraf.yale.edu/a-cross-cultural-look-at-posture-in-ehraf/.

Barton, J., R. Hine, and J. Pretty. "The Health Benefits of Walking in Greenspaces of High Natural and Heritage Value." Taylor & Francis, 2008. https://www.tandfonline.com/doi/full/10.1080/19438150903378425.

Bielinis, Ernest, Norimasa Takayama, Sergii Boiko, Aneta Omelan, and Lidia Bielinis. "The Effect of Winter Forest Bathing on Psychological Relaxation of Young Polish Adults." *Urban Forestry & Urban Greening*. Urban & Fischer, December 16, 2017. https://www.sciencedirect.com/science/article/abs/pii/S1618866717304296.

Braley, Pam. "The Vestibular System." *The Inspired Treehouse*, March 2014. https://theinspiredtreehouse.com/vestibular/.

Breit, Sigrid, Aleksandra Kupferberg, Gerhard Rogler, and Gregor Hasler. "Vagus Nerve as Modulator of the Brain–Gut Axis in Psychiatric and Inflammatory Disorders." *Frontiers*, February 1, 2018. https://www.frontiersin.org/articles/10.3389/fpsyt.2018.00044/full?fbclid=IwAR3PA3EFjHZPgy0zsChJWyJMyVGkKyPM7SN7UDb2vCTuOCl97Ob2SQabkRo.

Brito, L.B., D.R. Ricardo, D.S. Araújo, P.S. Ramos, J. Myers, and C.G. Araújo. "Ability to Sit and Rise from the Floor as a Predictor of All-Cause Mortality." *European Journal of Preventive Cardiology*. U.S. National Library of Medicine, 2012. https://pubmed.ncbi.nlm.nih.gov/23242910/.

Brown, Dick, Gaétan Chevalier, and Michael Hill. "Pilot Study on the Effect of Grounding on Delayed-Onset Muscle Soreness." Mary Ann Liebert, Inc., Publishers, March 2, 2010. https://www.liebertpub.com/doi/full/10.1089/acm.2009.0399.

Brown, Richard, et al. "Grounding after moderate eccentric contractions reduces muscle damage." Open Access Journal of Sports Medicine, September 2015. https://www.ncbi.nlm.nih.gov/pmc/articles/PMC4590684/.

Brownlee, Nancy, Martha Foster, Donald P. Griffith, and C. Eugene Carlton. "Controlled Inversion Therapy: An Adjunct to the Elimination of Gravity-Dependent Fragments

Bibliography

Following Extracorporeal Shock Wave Lithotripsy." *The Journal of Urology*, June 1990. https://www.auajournals.org/doi/abs/10.1016/S0022–5347%2817%2940196–0.

Buckthorpe, Matthew, Matthew Stride, and Francesco Della Villa. "Assessing and Treating Gluteus Maximus Weakness—A Clinical Commentary." *International Journal of Sports Physical Therapy*. Sports Physical Therapy Section, July 2019. https://www.ncbi.nlm.nih.gov/pmc/articles/PMC6670060/.

Coles, Nicholas A., Jeff T. Larsen, and Heather C. Lench. "A meta-analysis of the facial feedback literature: Effects of facial feedback on emotional experience are small and variable." *Psychological Bulletin*, 2019. Originally found at https://www.sciencedaily.com/releases/2019/04/190412094728.htm.

Creasy, S.A., R.J. Rogers, T.D. Byard, R.J. Kowalsky, and J.M. Jakicic. "Energy Expenditure During Acute Periods of Sitting, Standing, and Walking." *Journal of Physical Activity & Health*. U.S. National Library of Medicine, December 2015. https://pubmed.ncbi.nlm.nih.gov/26693809/.

Cuddy, Amy, Jack Schultz, and Nathan Fosse. "P-Curving a More Comprehensive Body of Research on Postural Feedback Reveals Clear Evidential Value for Power-Posing Effects: Reply to Simmons and Simonsohn." SAGE Journals, March 2018. https://journals.sagepub.com/eprint/CzbNAn7Ch6ZZirK9yMGH/full.

Dekker, Rebecca. "Evidence on: Birthing Positions." Evidence Based Birth®, June 29, 2020. https://evidencebasedbirth.com/evidence-birthing-positions/.

DiPietro, Loretta, Andrei Gribok, Michelle S. Stevens, Larry F. Hamm, and William Rumpler. "Three 15-Min Bouts of Moderate Postmeal Walking Significantly Improves 24-h Glycemic Control in Older People at Risk for Impaired Glucose Tolerance." *Diabetes Care*. American Diabetes Association, June 11, 2013. https://care.diabetesjournals.org/content/early/2013/06/03/dc13–0084.

Donovan, Francesca. "This Is How Much of Your Life You've Spent on the Toilet." Unilad, April 2018. https://www.unilad.co.uk/featured/this-is-how-much-of-your-life-youve-spent-on-the-toilet/.

Dov, Sikirov. "Comparison of Straining during Defecation in Three Positions: Results and Implications for Human Health." Digestive Diseases and Sciences. U.S. National Library of Medicine, 2003. https://pubmed.ncbi.nlm.nih.gov/12870773/.

Dunlop, Dorothy D., Jing Song, Jennifer M. Hootman, Michael C. Nevitt, Pamela A. Semanik, Jungwha Lee, Leena Sharma, et al. "One Hour a Week: Moving to Prevent Disability in Adults With Lower Extremity Joint Symptoms." *American Journal of Preventive Medicine*. Elsevier, March 20, 2019. https://www.sciencedirect.com/science/article/abs/pii/S0749379719300455.

Garrett, Gregory, et al. "Call Center Productivity Over 6 Months Following a Standing Desk Intervention." Taylor & Francis, December 2015. https://www.tandfonline.com/doi/full/10.1080/21577323.2016.1183534?scroll=top&needAccess=true.

Gnanalatha, R.A.H. "A Study on the Effect of Savasana and Suryanamaskara on Blood Pressure." Institute of Indigenous Medicine, 2007. http://192.248.16.117:8080/research/bitstream/70130/2532/1/Dr.R.A.H.Gnanalatha.pdf.

Gokhale, Esther, and Susan Adams. *8 Steps to a Pain-Free Back: Natural Posture Solutions for Pain in the Back, Neck, Shoulder, Hip, Knee, and Foot.* Chichester: Lotus Publishing, 2008.

Golay, Jane, Saraswathi Vedam, and Leo Sorger. "The Squatting Position for the Second Stage of Labor: Effects on Labor and on Maternal and Fetal Well-Being." Wiley Online Library. John Wiley & Sons, Ltd, April 2, 2007. https://onlinelibrary.wiley.com/doi/abs/10.1111/j.1523–536X.1993.tb00420.x.

Grant, Joshua, and Pierre Rainville. "Pain Sensitivity and Analgesic Effects of Mindful States in Zen Meditators: A Cross-Sectional Study." LWW. *Psychosomatic Medicine*, January 2009. https://journals.lww.com/psychosomaticmedicine/Abstract/2009/01000/Pain_Sensitivity_and_Analgesic_Effects_of_Mindful.17.aspx.

Healy, Genevieve N., et al. "Replacing sitting by standing or stepping: associations with cardio-metabolic risk biomarkers." *European Heart Journal*, July 2015. Originally accessed at https://www.sciencedaily.com/releases/2015/07/150730220021.htm.

Henson, Joseph, Melanie J. Davies, Danielle H. Bodicoat, Charlotte L. Edwardson, Jason M.R. Gill, David J. Stensel, Keith Tolfrey, David W. Dunstan, Kamlesh Khunti, and Thomas Yates. "Breaking Up Prolonged Sitting With Standing or Walking Attenuates the Postprandial Metabolic Response in Postmenopausal Women: A Randomized Acute Study." *Diabetes Care*. American Diabetes Association, November 30, 2015. https://care.diabetesjournals.org/content/early/2015/11/29/dc15–1240.

Hewes, Gordon W. "The Anthropology of Posture." *Scientific American*, 1957. https://www.scientificamerican.com/article/the-anthropology-of-posture/.

Howard, Jacqueline. "The US Suicide Rate Is Up 33% Since 1999, Research Says." CNN, June 21, 2019. https://www.cnn.com/2019/06/20/health/suicide-rates-nchs-study/index.html.

Jee, Yong-Seok. "The effect of inversion traction on pain sensation, lumbar flexibility and trunk muscles strength in patients with chronic low back pain." Isokinetics and Exercise Science, 2013. https://www.researchgate.net/publication/264742284_The_effect_of_inversion_traction_on_pain_sensation_lumbar_flexibility_and_trunk_muscles_strength_in_patients_with_chronic_low_back_pain.

Johansson, Marcus, Terry Hartig, and Henk Staats. "Psychological Benefits of Walking: Moderation by Company and Outdoor Environment." International Association of Applied Psychology. John Wiley & Sons, Ltd, August 4, 2011. https://iaap-journals.onlinelibrary.wiley.com/doi/abs/10.1111/j.1758–0854.2011.01051.x.

Katzmarzyk, P.T., and I.M. Lee. "Sedentary behaviour and life expectancy in the USA: a cause-deleted life table analysis." *British Medical Journal*, 2012. https://pubmed.ncbi.nlm.nih.gov/22777603/.

Kirsch, John M. *Shoulder Pain? The Solution & Prevention*. Morgan Hill, CA: Bookstand Publishing, 2019.

Knight A.P., and Baer M. "Get Up, Stand Up: The Effects of a Non-Sedentary Workspace on Information Elaboration and Group Performance." *Social, Psychological and Personality Science*, 2014. https://journals.sagepub.com/doi/abs/10.1177/1948550614538463.

Lee, I.M., and David Buchner. "The Importance of Walking to Public Health." Medicine and Science in Sports and Exercise. U.S. National Library of Medicine, 2008. https://pubmed.ncbi.nlm.nih.gov/18562968/.

Lee, Ingrid. "The Joy of Abundance." *Time*—Special Edition: The Power of Joy, 2020.

Li, Q., Morimoto K, Kobayashi M, et al. "Visiting a Forest, but Not a City Increases Human Natural Killer Activity and Expression of Anti-Cancer Proteins." *International Journal of Immunopathology and Pharmacology*, January 2008.

Li, Q., K. Morimoto, A. Nakadai, et al. "Forest Bathing Enhances Human Natural Killer Activity and Expression of Anti-Cancer Proteins." *International Journal of Immunopathology and Pharmacology*, April 2007.

Manjunath Prasad, K.S., Barbara A. Gregson, Gerard Hargreaves, Tiernan Byrnes, Philip Winburn and A. David Mendelow. "Inversion therapy in patients with pure single level lumbar discogenic disease: a pilot randomized trial." Disability and Rehabilitation, 2012. https://www.tandfonline.com/doi/abs/10.3109/09638288.2011.647231.

Mao, Gen-Xiang, Yong-Bao Cao, Xiao-Guang Lan, Zhi-Hua He, Zhuo-Mei Chen, Ya-Zhen Wang, Xi-Lian Hu, Yuan-Dong Lv, Guo-Fu Wang, and Jing Yan. "Therapeutic Effect of Forest Bathing on Human Hypertension in the Elderly." *Journal of Cardiology*. Elsevier, September 1, 2012. https://www.sciencedirect.com/science/article/pii/S0914508712001852.

Marcelo Campos, M.D. "Heart Rate Variability: A New Way to Track Well-Being." Harvard Health Blog, October 24, 2019. https://www.health.harvard.edu/blog/heart-rate-variability-new-way-track-well-2017112212789.

Mitchell, C., A. Adebajo, E. Hay, and A. Carr. "Shoulder pain: diagnosis and management in primary care." *British Medical Journal*, 2005. https://www.ncbi.nlm.nih.

Bibliography

gov/pmc/articles/PMC1283277/#:~:text=Self%20reported%20prevalence%20of%20
shoulder,with%20new%20shoulder%20pain%20annually.

Morris, J.N., J.A. Heady, P.A.B. Raffle, et al. "Coronary Heart Disease and Physical Activity of Work." *Lancet*, 1953. https://www.sciencedirect.com/science/article/abs/pii/S0140673653914950.

Müller, Erich, et al. "Effectiveness of Grounded Sleeping on Recovery After Intensive Eccentric Muscle Loading." *Frontiers in Physiology*, January 2019. https://www.ncbi.nlm.nih.gov/pmc/articles/PMC6360250/.

Mustian, Karen, et al. "Multicenter, randomized controlled trial of yoga for sleep quality among cancer survivors." *Journal of Clinical Oncology*, 2013.

Neethu, M.D. "Effectiveness of Savasana On Blood Pressure Among Patients with Hypertension—A Quasi Experimental Study." *International Journal of Research in Engineering, Science and Management*, 2020. https://www.ijresm.com/Vol.3_2020/Vol3_Iss2_February20/IJRESM_V3_I2_96.pdf.

Noro, Kageyu, Rani Lueder, Shunji Yamada, Goroh Fujimaki, Hideki Oyama, and Yuki Hashidate. "Revisiting Sitting Cross-Cultural Aspects of Seating." SAGE Journals, 2006. https://journals.sagepub.com/doi/abs/10.1177/154193120605000704?journalCode=proe.

Ober, Clinton, Stephen T. Sinatra, and Martin Zucker. *Earthing: the Most Important Health Discovery Ever!* Laguna Beach, CA: Basic Health Publications, 2014.

Ognibene, Grant T., Wilson Torres, Rie von Eyben, and Kathleen C. Horst. "Impact of a Sit-Stand Workstation on Chronic Low Back Pain." *Journal of Occupational and Environmental Medicine*: March 2016. https://journals.lww.com/joem/Citation/2016/03000/Impact_of_a_Sit_Stand_Workstation_on_Chronic_Low.11.aspx.

Olshansky, S. Jay, et al. "A Potential Decline in Life Expectancy in the United States in the 21st Century: NEJM." *New England Journal of Medicine*, March 17, 2005. https://www.nejm.org/doi/full/10.1056/NEJMsr043743#t=article.

Omidi, Abdollah, and Fatemeh Zargar. "Effect of Mindfulness-Based Stress Reduction on Pain Severity and Mindful Awareness in Patients with Tension Headache: a Randomized Controlled Clinical Trial." Nursing and Midwifery Studies. Kashan University of Medical Sciences, September 2014. https://www.ncbi.nlm.nih.gov/pmc/articles/PMC4332994.

Paavola, Mika, Antti Malmivaara, Simo Taimela, Kari Kanto, Jari Inkinen, Juha Kalske, Ilkka Sinisaari, Vesa Savolainen, Jonas Ranstam, and Teppo L.N. Järvinen. "Subacromial decompression versus diagnostic arthroscopy for shoulder impingement: randomised, placebo surgery controlled clinical trial." *British Medical Journal*, 2018. https://www.sciencedaily.com/releases/2018/07/180720092518.htm.

Papp, M.E., P. Lindfors, N. Storck, et al. "Increased heart rate variability but no effect on blood pressure from 8 weeks of hatha yoga—a pilot study." BioMed Central, 2013. https://doi.org/10.1186/1756-0500-6-59.

Passi, R., K.K. Doheny, Y. Gordin, H. Hinssen, and C. Palmer. "Electrical Grounding Improves Vagal Tone in Preterm Infants." *Neonatology*, 2017. https://www.karger.com/Article/Abstract/475744#.

Patel, Alpa V., Leslie Bernstein, Anusila Deka, Heather Spencer Feigelson, Peter T. Campbell, Susan M. Gapstur, Graham A. Colditz, and Michael J. Thun. "Leisure Time Spent Sitting in Relation to Total Mortality in a Prospective Cohort of US Adults." OUP Academic. Oxford University Press, July 22, 2010. https://academic.oup.com/aje/article/172/4/419/85345#639953.

Peper, Erik, Richard Harvey, Lauren Mason, and I-Mei Lin. "Do Better in Math: How Your Body Posture May Change Stereotype Threat Response." NeuroRegulation, 2018. http://www.neuroregulation.org/article/view/18396.

"Physical Activity." World Health Organization. November 26, 2020. https://www.who.int/news-room/fact-sheets/detail/physical-activity.

Pronk, N.P., A.S. Katz, M. Lowry, and J.R. Payfer. "Reducing occupational sitting time and improving worker health: the Take-a-Stand Project." Preventing Chronic Disease. 2011. https://www.ncbi.nlm.nih.gov/pmc/articles/PMC3477898/.

Raichlen, David A., Herman Pontzer, Theodore W. Zderic, Jacob A. Harris, Audax Z.P. Mabulla, Marc T. Hamilton, and Brian M. Wood. "Sitting, Squatting, and the Evolutionary Biology of Human Inactivity." PNAS. National Academy of Sciences, March 31, 2020. https://www.pnas.org/content/117/13/7115.

Rantanen, T., Guralnik J.M., Foley D., et al. "Midlife Hand Grip Strength as a Predictor of Old Age Disability." *Journal of the American Medical Association*, 1999. https://jamanetwork.com/journals/jama/fullarticle/188748.

Rettner, Rachael. "Prolonged Sitting Linked to Breast and Colon Cancers." LiveScience. Purch, May 30, 2013. https://www.livescience.com/35953-prolonged-sitting-raises-breast-colon-cancer-risk.html.

Rine, Rose Marie. "Vestibular Rehabilitation for Children." Seminars in hearing. Thieme Medical Publishers, August 2018. https://www.ncbi.nlm.nih.gov/pmc/articles/PMC6054578/.

Roe, Jenny, and Peter Aspinall. "The Restorative Benefits of Walking in Urban and Rural Settings in Adults with Good and Poor Mental Health." *Health & Place*. Pergamon, November 10, 2010. https://www.sciencedirect.com/science/article/abs/pii/S1353829210001322.

Santaella, Danilo, et al. "Yoga Relaxation (Savasana) Decreases Cardiac Sympathovagal Balance in Hypertensive Patients." *Medical Express*, 2014. https://cdn.publisher.gn1.link/medicalexpress.net.br/pdf/v1n5a04.pdf.

Sarno, John E. *Mind over Back Pain: A Radically New Approach to the Diagnosis and Treatment of Back Pain.* New York: Berkley Books, 1999.

Schmeer, Kammi K, and Aimee J. Yoon. "Home sweet home? Home physical environment and inflammation in children." Social Science Research, 2016. https://www.ncbi.nlm.nih.gov/pmc/articles/PMC5116303.

Searing, Linda. "The Big Number: The Average U.S. Adult Sits 6.5 Hours a Day. For Teens, It's Even More." *The Washington Post.* WP Company, April 28, 2019. https://www.washingtonpost.com/national/health-science/the-big-numberthe-average-us-adult-sits-65-hours-a-day-for-teens-its-even-more/2019/04/26/7c29e4c2−676a-11e9-a1b6-b29b90efa879_story.html.

"Sedentary Behavior Increases the Risk of Certain Cancers." OUP Academic. Oxford University Press, June 14, 2014. https://academic.oup.com/jnci/article/106/7/dju206/1010488.

Shuval, Kerem, et al. "Standing, Obesity, and Metabolic Syndrome." Mayo Clinic, 2015. https://www.mayoclinicproceedings.org/article/S0025−6196(15)00628-X/abstract.

Sinatra, S.T., J.L. Oschman, G. Chevalier, and D. Sinatra. "Electric Nutrition: The Surprising Health and Healing Benefits of Biological Grounding (Earthing)." Alternative Therapies in Health and Medicine, 2017. https://pubmed.ncbi.nlm.nih.gov/28987038/.

Tetley, M. "Instinctive sleeping and resting postures: an anthropological and zoological approach to treatment of low back and joint pain." *British Medical Journal*, 2000. https://www.ncbi.nlm.nih.gov/pmc/articles/PMC1119282/.

Thorp, A.A., B.A. Kingwell, N. Owen, and D.W. Dunstan. "Breaking up workplace sitting time with intermittent standing bouts improves fatigue and musculoskeletal discomfort in overweight/obese office workers." *Occupational and Environmental Medicine*, November 2014. https://pubmed.ncbi.nlm.nih.gov/25168375/.

Townsend, Joseph B., and Susan Barton. "The Impact of Ancient Tree Form on Modern Landscape Preferences." *Urban Forestry & Urban Greening*. Urban & Fischer, June 18, 2018. https://www.sciencedirect.com/science/article/pii/S1618866718301146.

Tyagi, A., and M. Cohen. "Yoga and heart rate variability: A comprehensive review of the literature." *International Journal of Yoga*, 2016. https://www.ncbi.nlm.nih.gov/pmc/articles/PMC4959333/.

Wilmot, E.G., C.L. Edwardson, F.A. Achana, M.J. Davies, T. Gorely, L.J. Gray, K. Khunti,

Bibliography

T. Yates, and S.J. Biddle. "Sedentary time in adults and the association with diabetes, cardiovascular disease and death: systematic review and meta-analysis." *Diabetologia*, 2012. https://pubmed.ncbi.nlm.nih.gov/22890825/.

Zautra, Alex J., Robert Fasman, Mary C. Davis, and Arthur D. (Bud) Craig. "The Effects of Slow Breathing on Affective Responses to Pain Stimuli: An Experimental Study." PAIN®. No longer published by Elsevier, January 15, 2010. https://www.sciencedirect.com/science/article/abs/pii/S0304395909005740.

Zheng H., N. Orsini, J. Amin, A. Wolk, V.T. Nguyen, and F. Ehrlich. "Quantifying the dose-response of walking in reducing coronary heart disease risk: meta-analysis." *European Journal of Epidemiology*, 2009. https://pubmed.ncbi.nlm.nih.gov/19306107/.

Index

225

Index

Index

Index